The Darkness Divine

The Darkness Divine

A Loving Challenge to My Faith

Kristen L. Harper

Skinner House Books
Boston

www.skinnerhouse.org

Printed in the United States

Cover art: "Breathe" by Cicely Carew
Cover design by Rebecca McEwen
Text design by Jeff Miller

print ISBN: 978-1-55896-868-4
eBook ISBN: 978-1-55896-869-1

6 5 4 3 2 1
25 24 23 22 21

Library of Congress Cataloging-in-Publication Data

Names: Harper, Kristen L, author.
Title: The darkness divine : a loving challenge to my faith / by Kristen L. Harper.
Description: Boston, Massachusetts : Skinner House Books, [2021] | Summary: "In an effort to continue the dialogue about race and resisting white supremacy culture, Unitarian Universalist minister Kristen L. Harper uses both poetry and prose to question how language, pictures, and iconography have been used to demean and dehumanize Black and Brown people"— Provided by publisher.
Identifiers: LCCN 2021005827 (print) | LCCN 2021005828 (ebook) | ISBN 9781558968684 (print) | ISBN 9781558968691 (ebook)
Subjects: LCSH: Racism–Religious aspects. | Race in art. | Race in language.
Classification: LCC BL65.R3 H25 2021 (print) | LCC BL65.R3 (ebook) | DDC 200.89—dc23
LC record available at https://lccn.loc.gov/2021005827
LC ebook record available at https://lccn.loc.gov/2021005828

Contents

Acknowledgments

In memory of Jay Harper,
my love and my constant support.

To the Black and brown women
who have struggled in our faith, in our world,
to be seen, to be heard, to be received.

To the memory of Danielle Gladd,
who always encouraged me to use my voice
and to empower our youth of color to love themselves.

To Lalitha and Rev. Dr. Abhi Janamanchi,
thank you for your accompaniment.
Without you, the journey would have been
too lonely to take.

For all the women pioneers to whom I owe so much:
Dianne Arakawa
Yvonne Seon
Adele Smith-Penniman
Shuma Chakravarty

Michelle W. Bentley
Patricia Jimenez
Toni Vincent
Marjorie Bowens-Wheatley
Alma Faith Crawford
Danielle Di Bona

For the community of Unitarian Universalists,
may you find the commitment to make manifest
your highest principle:
that your life is inextricably linked with all life,
not better, not worse, not superior, not inferior—
Glorious! Inherently worthy!

Introduction

I have been writing poetry for most of my life. For me, poetry is the language of the heart. It allows me to pour from my soul the experiences, emotions, and thoughts I would otherwise inarticulately try to explain. The poetry in this book explores new visions of blackness and darkness; it challenges readers to look at things differently, to recognize where they contribute to or are affected by racist language; it provides a peek into the struggles of Black and brown communities and lifts up the beauty, resilience, and defiance of Black people, Indigenous people, and people of color (BIPOC). These poems attempt to provide some of the context and history that sparked their creation.

I was raised with the belief that all people are one—equally worthy, equally deserving.

One Being

We are one being—
born from the same dark mother
blessed in equal measure;
worthy of the intense love of the Goddess.
Over hundreds of thousands of years, we became lost.
We were taken from our birthplace
and forced into a vast new world,
over lands now separated by water and deserts not
    once there;
adapting to the strange environments in which we
    found ourselves.
We grew and our bodies changed to deal with the cold,
the mountains, the plains,
to deal with being migrants in strange new lands;
with new foods, new predators, new opportunities;
to deal with the oppressive enslavement of those
who had no right to own us or the land which they
    made us work;
to fit into a world where freedom was promised but
    not always fulfilled.
Our one being was splintered, fractured by those
    distorted by greed and power,
creating distinctions they used to divide and conquer.
And so we hunkered in our tribes, defending our
    position,
creating differences where there were none,
changing rituals, customs, and traditions to fit with
    our new homes,
keeping old ways secret in songs, dance, and prayer,
far away from the dark mother who bore us.

One day when life fades, and the folly and illusion of
    our separateness is unmasked,
we will merge back into our one being.
Until then, the ache of our great loss will haunt us.

With the naivety and optimism of youth, I embraced the
idea of the inherent worth and dignity of every person and went
about trying to affirm this in those who I believed desperately
needed to embody this ideal. As I volunteered with Black and
brown women isolated by the AIDS crisis, domestic violence,
and white supremacy, I recognized the saving grace that the
faith of my childhood could be to those whose beauty and stories were hidden beneath the crushing weight of punishing
dogma and the generational effects of racial inequality.

PRECIOUS BEINGS

These beautiful brown bodies
ravaged by years of abuse and neglect
sought release in the streets, from needles
filled with poisonous oblivion,
from strangers who would use them for personal gain.
They separated their spirit from the containers holding
    their life
and held their breath, closed off their hearts
and thought they had laid down their precious worth.
AIDS, they were told, was a punishment from God,
retribution for a life they did not ask for

and would have gladly exchanged.
Abandoned by friends and families,
cast out by ministers and priests,
many died alone, on the streets, in flop houses,
	in hospitals
surrounded by cold, unforgiving righteousness.
Others found their way to compassionate caregivers
who gently shepherded their last breaths into the
	world beyond.
These beautiful brown souls
were worthy of the loving God that wraps divine
	tendrils around us
and never lets us go.
These beautiful brown women
did not know how precious they really were.

In seminary, I quickly discovered that my faith community struggles with the idea of the inherent worth and dignity of Black, brown, and other marginalized people. Like many religious communities, Unitarian Universalists have tried to tackle sexism, racism, homophobia, transphobia, heterosexism, ableism, and classism—and yet, like other well-intentioned faith communities, we find ourselves ensnared by white supremacy. We continue to make mistakes, traumatizing and pushing away people who would add richness and depth to our movement.

Many white Unitarian Universalists ask themselves, "Why are there not more Black and brown people in our Association?" Because Unitarian Universalism is a liberal faith, many of its white members believe that the problem is "out there" with other people, and not within their own doors or hearts. The Association repels people of color because of its largely white membership, completely unaware of the racist language they use to talk about and address BIPOC.

The poems in this book are full of joy and hope, suffering and sorrow, anger and resentment, survival and resistance. My goal is to expose some of the language of racism, explore the negative imagery of darkness, and name how both impact the lives of many Black and brown people. While my poems do not speak for all people of color, I know well the hearts and minds and experiences of white people. I intend to open a door to narratives that differ from the dominant one, to question how language—broadly defined in words, pictures, iconography, and body language—has been used to demean, dismiss, and dehumanize Black and brown people. I want to continue the dialogue about race and, through poetry, begin to recognize and resist the white supremacy culture in which we find ourselves.

Rising to Thrive

They say it is biological,
but we are biological siblings,
99.9 percent identical.
They say it is character—a drive to succeed, to
        conquer, to consume,

But I do not see much character in their greed,
    oppression, and warring ideology.
They say the opportunities are there for everyone
    to grasp,
but broken treaties, broken promises, broken lives
reveal the lie of equal access.
And yet still we rise,
again and again
pushing through the barriers meant to hold us back,
    hold us down.
Still we rise, with hopeful hearts and hurting souls,
coming ever closer to the lives we dream about.
Still we rise, creating a wake that others might draft in.
Still we rise, knowing that one day, with straight backs
and proud heads, we shall thrive.

In 1976, Robert B. Moore, author and member of the Council on Interracial Books for Children, in his essay "Racism in the English Language" wrote, "An integral part of any culture is its language. Language not only develops in conjunction with society's historical, economic and political evolution, but also reflects that society's attitude and thinking. Language not only expresses ideas and concepts, but actually shapes thought."

White culture determines the language of our society and therefore shapes societal thinking. Although white people also appropriate certain words and phrases from other cultures, white-dominated language continues to justify the superiority of white people and the oppression of Black and brown people. The language we use to describe people and communities of color, as well as the language we use to dismiss Black and brown concerns, impacts how the majority thinks and acts toward people of color.

For two and a half decades, I have searched for positive, empowering imagery of darkness and blackness that can counteract coded or indirect racist language. Along the way, I have written poems and meditations that purposely question assumptions about communities of color by centering the beauty, strength, and resilience of Black and brown people — and praising darkness itself. I have also explored certain words and phrases used to demean and dismiss the reality of Black and brown lives.

The language of racism comes in many forms: the negative imagery of the words *black* and *dark*, which co-mingle with white people's negative views of Black and brown communities; how God and Jesus are viewed as white; how the feelings and experiences of people of color are demeaned; how the real pain and trauma of Black and brown people and communities are dismissed; and the images and stereotypes used to portray people of color.

In my poems and essays, I often use the terms *Black and brown* or *people of color* to describe the people I have known and with whom I have been in relationship who belong to Black, Asian, Indigenous, and Latinx communities. My work doesn't attempt to speak *for* all of them, but rather *to* them, as they have always been part of my web of existence and have been wrestling with similar white supremacist manifestations with a grace and power that I admire.

This book of poetry is designed for all readers but centers Black and brown perspectives. It offers dark imagery and language and reflects on what the latter might change in us. These words provide a chance to explore how everyone's spiritual lives might benefit from some imaginative and curious soul-pouring.

Say It Loud, "I'm Black and I'm Proud!"

A white member of one of the congregations I served once asked me, "Why do you use the term 'Black' to refer to yourself? I don't see black as a person—it's a color. Besides, you are multiracial." I really didn't wish to engage in a deep discussion about self-determination and identity development, so I responded, "You may not see me as Black, but most of the world judges me, reacts to me, and responds to me based solely on my skin color." Before I can even open my mouth, before a hello is even said, my skin color contains a host of stereotypes and projected value assessments I am expected to overcome or confirm.

As a teenager, I felt conflicted about calling myself Black. My classmates would often talk about being Italian American, Irish American, English, Polish, or simply "American." Why did I have to claim an entire continent with over 3,000 ethnicities, none of which claimed me? The African American experience was certainly one to which I could relate—

the fear and hatred, the internal and external barriers, and the stereotypes and lowered expectations. But I was not raised in an African American family. I gained my cultural knowledge through observation and reading, not lived experience. But the truth is, I'm Black and I'm proud!

For me, being a Black person connects me with the people and history of my African lineage and places me squarely in a position of power, beauty, and pride. The Black Power movement of the 1960s and 1970s advocated racial pride, equality, and community autonomy for people of African descent. Trinidadian-born Stokely Carmichael (Kwame Ture), chair of the Student Nonviolent Coordinating Committee and leader of the Black Panther Party for Self-Defense, is credited with bringing Black Power into public awareness during the 1966 March Against Fear. During the peaceful march from Memphis, Tennessee, to Jackson, Mississippi, a white man shot and injured civil rights activist James Meredith. The march continued and ended in a mass rally where Carmichael spoke the indelible words, "What we need is Black power." Chants of "Black Power!" filled the air, and a movement was born.

While many in the Black Power movement were unafraid to use force to protect their community from police and white violence, most white people failed to understand that the Black Power movement wasn't about violence but rather the empowerment of Black people—to know our worth, own our beauty, develop self-respect and pride, help one another rise economically and educationally, and shield ourselves against the forces of white supremacy. Members of the movement worked to feed, clothe, and educate Black adults and children. They stressed the beauty of Pan-Africanism and encouraged the community to have pride in our natural hair, the color of our skin, and the ways in which we differed from the larger white society. The Black Power movement taught us about Pan-African customs, encouraged us to wear African clothes and colors, and urged us to develop new African American traditions to strengthen Black family and community ties.

I was born after the height of the Black Power movement, two weeks before the police murdered Fred Hampton. My white adoptive mother introduced me to Hampton as well as Stokely Carmichael, Huey P. Newton, Bobby Seale, and Angela Davis. She believed that I should know about both civil rights and Black Power activists, so I grew up reading about Rev. Dr. Martin Luther King Jr. and Malcolm X. I believe she understood that my growing up in a white family in a white town while attending a white school meant that I needed Black pride and Black power in my life.

In an effort to compensate for the racism she knew I would experience, my adoptive mother filled my head with the beauty, strength, and resiliency of Blackness as well as many unflattering stereotypes about white people: Black people had rhythm and soul; white people couldn't dance and had no rhythm. Black people had survived centuries of discrimination and continued to fight for equality and self-determination; white people were weak and needed protection. Black people were intelligent and clever; white people were clueless about the real world. Whenever racism overwhelmed me, she would say, "Just wait until you meet other Black people. You'll see." I internalized her messages so deeply that I never once wanted to be white, and was surprised when one of the two other Black girls in my school asked me, "Don't you hate being Black?" But it never occurred to me. I loved my Blackness. I was the descendant of the strongest race alive. Because of my adoptive mother's efforts to help me establish my Black identity, I often wondered what was wrong with me that other people *couldn't* appreciate my beauty. Being Black is a gift with a long and proud legacy.

THE STUFF IN MY BONES

I do not move alone.
I move with the Queens and Kings of Africa,
the artisans and wise women, architects, and
    medicine men.
The builders and shapers of America,
the truth-speakers and the soul-transformers
of a nation separated but not divided.
My beauty stretches back to the beginning,
an emanation of love, wisdom, and strength.
Born from the glorious blackness of creation,
my pride earned in the straight backs and raised
    chins
not bowed by the lash of the whip, the kick of the
    boot,

or the slap of a hand that will never master my spirit.
I move with the souls of women who never gave up,
who bore and buried life,
dug up and rebuilt foundations of movements
that altered laws and lives.
The doers and the creators of change.
These Black and brown women
who carried communities on their shoulders
were the invisible heroes in science, math, and
    education.
They were nurses, doctors, paramedics, lab techs,
    and aides,
cleaners and chefs, nannies and maids,
mothers and aunts, grandmothers and sisters,
neighbors and friends.
They were more than silent shadows, hidden figures.
I move with them in my heart, in my soul, in my
    bones.

2

A Theology of Darkness

The Darkness Divine

God resides in depths of darkness
    as in the light of sunbeams.
The moon shines brighter surrounded by night
    and life is secure in the black waters of the womb.
As the night sky littered with stars demonstrates
      again and again,
there is beauty in darkness and beauty in light—
    one no more brilliant then the other,
    one no more necessary than the other,
    one always complementing the other.
Without the heated darkness of the Universe,
splitting neutrons, electrons, and protons from atoms,
life and light would never be.
The task for us today
    is to recognize God in both—
To see the divine in the rich brown earth,
    the textured black walnut,
    as well as the white snow and the pale pink jellyfish.
To see the sacred in the panther and the swan.
To embrace the dignity of the Black Madonna,
    as it is embodied in the Virgin Mary.

The task for us today
is to look into the multifaceted colors of the onyx
and see the miraculous spectrum of color
produced in the prism of a diamond.

To begin the dismantling of our racist language, we first need a new theology of darkness—a new way to relate to the darkness, blackness, and brownness that surrounds us, and to the people whose skin is often reflected in our disempowering language. Poetry can help us cultivate a different relationship with and to blackness and darkness. In the darkness exists a time for rest, a time of regeneration and healing, a time of safety and nourishment, and a time of letting go to relax in God's embrace.

As a spiritual humanist, I believe that which we call God—the energetic force of love and creation—is within us and around us, connecting and empowering us as we move toward one another and through the world. While there are many definitions of theology, I lead with a theology rooted in relationship with one another, the earth, God, the spirit of life, all that is holy, and the higher good that can occur when we recognize and affirm our interdependence. This relationship, both conscious and unconscious, impacts how we operate in the world, how we view and treat others, and how we respond to injustices in which we play a part.

When beginning to explore new concepts, it is often helpful to study their etymology. At least two root words point to the modern-day understanding of *black*. The Old English word *blaec* signified "absolute dark, absorbing all light, the color of soot or coal." And then there is *blac*, which signified "bright, shining, glittering, pale." It is unclear, however, if either term was used to describe people with dark skin. In Old English, the word for the color black was *sweart*. It resembles the late fifteenth-century *swarthy*, which meant "of dark skin." In Old French, Italian, and Spanish, the root word *blac* meant "pale, wan, colorless or albino."

Sometime in the 1300s, *black* became associated with sin and sorrow in English-speaking countries. By the mid-1400s, when the Doctrine of Discovery was first legitimized and the colonization of African nations encouraged, *black* was used to mean "terrible, wicked, without moral or spiritual light."

Dum Diversas, or "Doctrine of Discovery," began as a 1452 papal decree issued to King Alfonso V of Portugal. In essence, it declared the inferiority of all non-Christians, specifically Africans and their lands. Steven Newcomb, a member of the Shawnee and Lenape tribes and the co-founder and co-director of the Indigenous Law Institute, explained in his paper, "Five Hundred Years of Injustice: The Legacy of Fifteenth Century Religious Prejudice," that "Pope Nicholas directed King Alfonso V to 'capture, vanquish, and subdue the saracens [a Crusades-era term used for Arabs and Muslims], pagans, and other enemies of Christ,' to 'put them into perpetual slavery,' and 'to take all their possessions and property.'" Trying to evade Islamic traders, Portugal embraced this decree and spread their dominion along the western coast of Africa, accelerating the enslavement and selling of native Africans.

By the time Christopher Columbus encountered the "New World" fifty years later, Europe had fully embraced the tradition of discovery and conquest. Upon Columbus's return to Europe, Ferdinand and Isabel, the monarchs of Spain, requested Pope Alexander VI to reiterate the previous decree and grant Spain "the right to conquer lands which Columbus had already found, as well as any land which Spain might 'discover' in the future." Pope Alexander VI added his desire for the "discovered" people to be "subjugated and brought to the faith itself."

These documents gave permission to European Christians to enslave, dehumanize, torture, rape, and murder the indigenous people of Africa, Asia, the Caribbean, and the Americas. According to Steven Newcomb, these two papal decrees enforced—and Christian nations embraced—that Indigenous people were "the lawful spoil and prey of their civilized conquerors."

In order to justify their greed, the Portuguese, by designating Africans and other Indigenous people as "terrible, wicked, without moral or spiritual light," uncivilized, and enemies of Christ, were able to strip them of their humanity and, I believe, marked the beginnings of the denigration of blackness and of darkness.

On August 25, 1619, the *White Lion* docked at Point Comfort (now known as Fort Monroe National Monument) in Hampton, Virginia, packed with Black bodies—the first recorded arrival of enslaved Africans in America. On the 400th anniversary of this day, Black descendants of enslaved Africans organized a ceremony of healing and reconciliation at Fort Monroe. Communities across the United States were asked to ring bells at 3:00 PM for four minutes to mark the 400 years since that infamous day.

That First Day, That Hour, That Minute

How do we mark that first day, that hour, that minute
the *White Lion* docked at a point that would be of no
    comfort
to the twenty enslaved Africans chained in her
    bowels—
heralds of a coming storm of millions
whose bodies would break through soil and rock to
build an America that could never fully embrace its
    progenitors.
How do we mark that day, that hour, that minute,
that foreshadowed the centuries to come of
    degradation and violence,
of attempts to separate the soul and spirit
from the deep well of Black lives.
How do we mark that day, that hour, that minute
four hundred years ago, when the first drop of
    African sweat

co-mingled with the earth's warmth, planting the seeds
of a new culture, a new way of life, a new heartbeat
into the fabric of a new world—
when the roots of freedom sparked deep underground
and spread, from generation to generation,
blossoming into resistance and resilience.
So today we will ring bells of sorrow, bells of grief,
bells of atonement.
We will ring out the ghosts of those lost in the middle
    passages,
lost to the whips and deprivation, lost to the lynchings
    and the bullets,
lost to the prisons and the chains of racism.
Today we will ring bells,
so that tomorrow we may ring in freedom,
ring in liberation,
ring in peace.

As a student of religion and race for many decades, I have been concerned about the consistent equating of darkness and blackness with negative qualities such as sin and despair. Our connection to the divine is a deeply personal, driving force. Continuing to associate *black* and *dark* with "evil" or "the absence of God" has only contributed to fear, dehumanization, and violence toward Black and brown people. A new relationship with blackness and darkness should include lifting up the creation possible within the dark and its empowering and nurturing qualities.

CREATION IN THE DARKNESS

In the beginning, there was darkness, a blackness that
  covered all,
comprising the building blocks of creation—
the nutrients and nurturing needed to birth the world.
This dark womb pushed out the light that released
  the heavens
and cradled the planets and stars adorning the
  universe;
it formed the darkened earth from which all life
  emerged
and to which all life returns when our bodies take
  their final breath.
It is the same darkness that shelters us from an
  unrelenting sun;
that calls animals to a safe hibernation;
that protects the germination of seed and bulb.
Darkness signals an end to the hectic chaos of our days,
and lulls us to sleep and revitalization so that we can
  face the next challenge.
There is peace in darkness, and mystery, and the
  unknown,
And if we can rest in its grace, cease fighting to
  control it,
we just might see in it the face of God.

Darkness has almost always been considered negative. In
Old English, the word *deorc* meant "without light, obscure,
gloomy, or sad, cheerless, sinister, wicked." Phrases like "dark

mood" and "dark night of the soul" only reinforce our negative feelings. We are taught to fear the dark—that all the monsters and demons come out in the dark. But those who hurt others under the guise of "battling monsters" do so as much in the daylight as in the night. The light does not hide war, famine, abuse, greed, torture, or any other kind of violence. Light does not hide our sadness or depression, our loneliness or our despair. Darkness may even be a salve to the intensity of the light.

Those who follow seasonal rituals have attempted to reclaim the "dark times" as an important part of the natural order of things, but still often focus heavily on the return of light and the sun. Apart from a period of waiting for the sun to return, the dark is rarely celebrated for what it brings to our lives. Relearning to appreciate the darkness takes intention and practice.

BRAVE IN THE DARK

Why must my heart break at the setting of the sun,
when darkness comes with loving hands to draw me
        into sleep?
Is not the blanket of the night as warm as morning rays?
Are not the stars that fill the dark sky connecting me
        to the world
    of dreams and imagination?
Does not the blue-blackness of night's expanse deserve
        our awe and admiration?

Without the glare of light, I can finally see—
   see beyond the masks, beyond the robes that hide
      all imperfections,
   see the tears and rips and ragged scars
   that mark the truth hidden in the light.
Yes, it takes sharp eyes to uncover the life beneath
      the dark ocean
   but the yellows and oranges and reds contained
      there
   are just as magnificent as those on land.
The light does not reveal more to me than the dark.
Truth is, my heart is already broken and the sun sees
      it not.
The blazing fire in the sky does not allow me to speak
      more easily,
to name my suffering and bask in its flare.
   But in the dark, my tears can fall in relief.
   In the dark my scars fade and I can sense healing.
   In the dark I find freedom and can finally be brave.

Questions for Discussion

1. What is your relationship to God, to the holy, to nature, to humanity?

2. What is your relationship to black, brown, and darkness?

3. What impact does the negative use of the words *dark* and *black* have on you?

4. What is some positive imagery of darkness and blackness?

5. What words might you use to replace *dark* and *black* to describe your mood or experience?

6. How might a positive understanding of *black* and *dark* deepen your relationship with the holy?

    White readers: How might your understanding of *black* and *dark* deepen your relationship with people who are Black or brown?

    Black and brown readers: How might your understanding of *black* and *dark* change how we perceive ourselves?

1. Write three sentences where you replace the word *dark* or *black* for other descriptive terms. For example, instead of "I was in a dark mood," try writing "I was in a foul mood."

2. Create a poem where you describe the beauty and/or power of blackness or the dark.

3. Imagine God as a dark, comforting, healing, creative blanket. Compose a prayer or meditation where this holy darkness is the central theme.

4. As you go about your week, seek positive black, brown, and dark imagery, and record it in a journal.

3

I Found God Inside Myself—and She's Black

Central figures in Christian theology are often depicted as white. Even though many in my faith tradition have moved away from Christianity, they still bring with them and unwittingly promote the white supremacy embedded in its iconography and prose. Although the majority of the world's people are Black or brown, the image of white saviors puts communities of color in a paternalistic relationship with the holy. Through poetry I ask, "What if God were a brown woman?" "What if Jesus were a Black man?" How would this reframing change our relationship with the sacred and with the BIPOC within whom the divine is seldom recognized?

For Christians and other theists, theology embraces a relationship with God, or God and Jesus. For instance, in predominantly white congregations, Black and brown people often do not have the image of God reflected in their bodies. In 1996, I saw the Ntozake Shange play, "For Colored Girls

Who've Considered Suicide When the Rainbow Was Enuf." In the final act, the women sing, "I found God inside myself and I loved her." As the words vibrated around the room, I understood the holy in a visceral way. Until then, I had rejected all ideas of God—particularly a white male figure on high, puppeteering his creation in some grand but unknown-to-us plan. For me, this God must be a sadist, condemning so many people to suffering and punishing his Black and brown creations for some imagined slight. Or perhaps playing a game to find out what it takes to break a people down, or demanding sacrifices to test the depth of faith. I had decided that if there was a God, then I did not wish to be in his heaven.

Until that moment, sitting in that crowded South Side Chicago theater, I felt that I was missing something. As Shange writes in her play, "I waz missing somethin, somethin so important, somethin promised, a layin on of hands, fingers near my forehead, strong, cool, movin, makin me whole, sense pure, all the gods comin into me, layin me open to myself." A couple years ago, a friend gave me a T-shirt that read, "I Met God and She's Black." I always smile inside when I wear it. The idea that there is a Black Goddess who reflects my divinity is a powerful and empowering concept.

IN THE ARMS OF BLACKNESS

Divine Blackness,
It is into your embrace I fall to rest
when the world seems too cruel to carry.

Your ebony arms encircle my body heavy with grief,
trembling with fear, weary with hopelessness.
I see my tears reflected in the lines of your brown
  face,
ancient and timeless, warm and understanding.
I feel your strong fingers on my curly brown head,
cradling my brokenness, blessing me with a call to
  healing.
You who sheltered Hagar and Ishmael.
You who cried with each enslaved mother whose child
  was torn from her breast,
breathed with your children with each lash of the
  whip,
held our hands as our bodies were violated again and
  again.
You who shepherded Harriet and Frederick to freedom.
You who sat with Rosa
and walked through angry white mobs with Charlayne
  Hunter-Gault.
It is your strong feet that carry me forward when
  strength eludes me.
It is your power I draw upon when feeling powerless.
My Black goddess,
you strip all my defenses, all my pretenses,
and bare my naked soul to your radiant joy.

I Met God and She's Black

It was late summer. The air was still warm, but the
cooling darkness was just setting upon me. I was
sitting on the beach, listening to the waves and

29

digging my toes into the heated sand, when she sat down next to me. I was not frightened but my soul began to vibrate, activated by the smell of earth and pine, out of place for where we were and at the same time completely right and familiar. I looked at her round hips and stomach, her thick thighs, and rich brown skin. I was drawn to the brilliant radiance of her night. There were no burning bushes or disembodied voices—just a beautiful smile and ancient eyes that looked knowingly into mine.

We sat for a while in silence until I could no longer hold the intensity of the energy flowing toward me.

"Will I see it end?" I asked, knowing in an instant that she understood—the end of injustice, the end of war, the end of hatred, the end of the earth.

Her voice came not from her mouth but from deep within me, quiet and fierce, sad but resolved. "No," she said—the response I had known but was dreading. I was silent for a while, struggling with my sadness and disappointment, until she gently affirmed, "But you already knew that." Yes, I thought to myself. I already knew that.

"It is not what I wanted for you—for any of you."

In frustration, I replied, "Then why must it be so? What did we do?"

She remained silent as my anger swirled around me. Then she told me to breathe. "You do what you want," she said. "You do what you think you must.

You divide and order, you demonize and scapegoat, you take and you destroy."

"You made us this way," I retorted, expecting her to deny it, to explain evolution, to bring up free will.

"Yes," she replied, "I did." I sat there digesting her honesty, seeing the deep lines in her face reflect the sorrow of centuries of her creations deconstructing her magnificent dreams.

I had to ask, "Is there another life? Another place that's easier, that's filled with joy and happiness? Will we find peace in death?"

She did not answer my question. Instead she replied, "Is not heaven love? Is not the grasp of a baby's hand joy? Is there not peace in the quiet of the forest, in the arms of your friends, in the stars twinkling at night?

"Spread compassion. Build caring communities. Cross barriers. Tear down prisons. Lay on this precious earth. Do not let your fears divide you— from any being. Heaven is not easy. It is not found in death.

"Breathe," she said again, and took my hands in her large, rough ones. The frantic energy between us dissipated. She smiled again. I felt her voice swell from deep within me and I knew my worth.

I have often found myself confused by the images of Jesus as a European man with light-colored hair and blue eyes. The historical Jesus is said to have lived and offered ministry in an area spanning North Africa and the Middle East. And yet the images of Jesus do not reflect that. What if Jesus were a Black man? Or a brown woman? Would his identity invalidate what he taught? Would she still be worshipped by millions of people around the world? If we portrayed Jesus as he most likely appeared — brown-skinned, dark-haired, perhaps curly, but definitely brown-eyed — would that change the way we perceive Pan-African, Indigenous, and Latinx communities?

Brown in All Her Glory

That image of Jesus there,
that image of a thin white man with dirty blond hair
cascading down his shoulders,
with bright blue eyes that hold no sympathy for me,
no understanding of my pain, my experiences, my
    reality—
does not move me.
I do not see my life reflected in his countenance.
Even the stigmatic flow from his hands and feet
does not reflect the rivers of blood my people have
    shed.
It is the bodies of Harriette Vyda Simms Moore,
Marsha P. Johnson, Berta Isabel Cáceres Flores,
    Malala Yousafzai,
that I see carrying my cross, bleeding for my sins.
In their gaze, I see empathy and determination,
    sacrifice and love,
an understanding that is not ephemeral, but bone deep;

that stretches through time—past, present, and
    future.
They were baptized by life, by war, by hatred, by fire.
They did not simply welcome the poor and
    oppressed,
they were the embodiment of resistance born from
    injustice.
For organizing the uneducated, the poor, the
    oppressed, she died.
To expand the rights of and understanding of what it
    is to be a woman, she died.
Trying to wake people up to the destruction of our
    beloved earth, she died.
For the chance to go to school and be equal, she was
    shot in the head.
Their ministries spanned more than three years,
    and yet there were miracles;
their parables were just as powerful, their lives just
    as holy,
their love too expansive to be contained in this
    world.
Empty of hope, it is at their feet I fall in gratitude
    and in grief,
finding strength in theirs, finding love in their deep,
    blazing, brown eyes.

Christian scriptures give only a scant description of Jesus.
He was born in Bethlehem and raised in Nazareth, a town
formerly known as Palestine. In *Revelations*, Jesus is described

as having hair like wool and feet the color of burnished bronze, refined as in a furnace. Though it is unclear if it was the texture or color of his hair was like wool, his burnished, bronze feet were clearly not the pale white of most portrayals. Many Jewish people have tight, blond curls, so it is possible that Jesus had the same. Jesus was a Palestinian Jewish man living in Galilee. He most likely resembled an Arab man, not the Nordic god as he is most often depicted.

Sometime during the Middle Ages, the image of Jesus changed from a brown-skinned man with a beard and dark eyes to a clean-shaven, dirty blonde-haired man with blue eyes. Speculation about why this happened varies. *HuffPost* Black Voices editor Taryn Finley writes that Christians of the Middle Ages "didn't like the idea of Jesus having Jewish features, even though he was Jewish."

Finley also references the BBC television series *Son of God*, during which media personality Franchesca Ramsey speculates that "Biblical passages that referred to lightness symbolizing purity, and darkness symbolizing sin and evil, played into how people perceived Jesus' appearance. . . . Again, we see this narrative of [dark-skinned] people being bad, thus needing to be tamed or killed in order to confirm the good or white standard." Finley concludes, "[Ramsey] touches on the notion of white supremacy being used in Christianity to colonize and control before and during slavery," noting that "white power structures excluded images with a darker complexion to spread racial bias."

Would it really matter if Jesus were brown and Jewish? Would his words be less significant if his skin was the color of rich chocolate? Would his darkness negate the compassion he bestowed upon the soul of a world so desperately in need? Would you not appreciate his power to heal the wounded heart, bring people together, provide hope, and promise salvation if his hands were the color and texture of walnuts? Can we not imagine a god bringing forth beautiful darkness to shine the fire of justice upon the least of these, to upend the marginalization of his people? Would it really matter if the vessel that connected us to the promise of life eternal was burnt sienna or mahogany? Darkness resides in the depths of Bethlehem, in the sands of Jerusalem, in the sea of Galilee. Why not in the one who moved through and around the holy sites, blessing them? If Jesus were Black, would his love be any less transforming?

In US culture, the default assumption is that God is white and male. What would it mean if God were a woman, a person of color, or nonbinary? Would women's bodies then be seen as temples of love and not just vessels for bearing children or objects for use and abuse? Would we be free to explore who we are and how we want to be in the world without being confined to rigid gender roles that trap us all in unattainable opposites? How would these identities change the way we think and speak about God—not only in our own hearts but in our public worship?

THE 23RD PSALM REVISITED

Love is my shepherd;
I shall not want.
Love embraces all of me in her green pastures;

Love cradles me in her still waters;
Love restores my soul.
Love compels me towards justice
for the world's sake.
Even though I walk through life
with death ever before me,
I fear it not.
For I walk not alone;
Love is with me.
Her deep roots and dark wings,
they comfort me.
Love brings me to the table
in the presence of those with whom I am at discord.
Her rich brown hands bless me with the oil of
    compassion;
my heart overflows.
Surely, goodness and mercy
shall follow me all the days of my life
and I will dwell in the arms of Love
my whole life long.
Amen!

QUESTIONS FOR DISCUSSION

1. In what ways does the perceived color of Jesus lead to the further oppression of Black and brown communities?

2. With what images of Jesus and of God were you raised, and how do you think these images shaped your understanding of these figures?

3. How might your relationship to the holy change if God and Jesus were Black or brown? How would it change if God and Jesus were a woman of color?

4. What characteristics of the divine comfort and empower you? Are these characteristics limited to one race or ethnicity?

1. Research the life and work of Harriette Vyda Simms Moore, Marsha P. Johnson, Berta Isabel Cáceres Flores, and Malala Yousafzai.

2. Educate yourself about Mahatma Gandhi, Rev. Dr. Martin Luther King Jr., César Chavez, Nelson Mandela, and Wanbli Ohitika. Learn about other Black, Indigenous, Asian, and Latinx cultural workers and how their lives might be examples to Unitarian Universalism in embracing a liberation-based theology.

3. List the underlying themes and characteristics of these exemplars' lives and how their cultural location as BIPOC empowered them to do the work of justice.

4. Write a story, essay, poem, or meditative reading about spiritual liberation that centers a Jesus of color who embodies the themes and characteristics you discovered.

4

I'm Not Angry—
I am Fierce!

The Angry Black Person stereotype has been used to dismiss Black voices and concerns. If we are just angry, then white people don't have to listen or pay attention to us. Recognizing our right to be angry, speak out, and honor our anger and tears as survival and pain-release tools are important steps in dismantling the suffocating white supremacist expectation of silence.

The Angry Black Woman (or Angry Black Man) label is one of many racist ways language is used to demean Black people. Whenever Black people name the discrimination we experience, we are labeled "angry," which focuses attention not on the micro- or macroaggressions, or the gaslighting that whiteness has weaponized, but on the Black person who is bravely naming their truth.

In one of my first sermons on racism, I described several incidents of being pulled over for Driving While Black. I explained that, each time, the officer did not give me a ticket but questioned why I was in a predominantly white area or asked about the expiration date of tags and emission stickers that were clearly still valid. Although I then went on to talk about the inherent worth and dignity Unitarian Universalists hold sacred, and how it is up to us to create the Beloved Community here on earth with one another, members of the congregation still accused me of being angry.

Labeling Black people as angry is a way to manipulate us into thinking that what we are experiencing and feeling is all in our head. For a long time, this gaslighting tactic upset me—I didn't want to be perceived as angry. It was love, not hate, that drove my attempts to expose the racism I was experiencing—love for my faith, other BIPOC, and myself, and the desire for love from others for all of who I am.

In *Eloquent Rage: A Black Feminist Discovers Her Superpower*, writer, scholar, and activist Brittney Cooper writes, "Black anger, black rage, black distress over injustice is seen as, one: unreasonable and outsized; and two: as a thing that must be neutralized and contained quickly." Black people are labeled "bad and . . . ungrateful for being angry."

I have come to see anger as a survival tool—a way to not simply stuff all the ignorance, hatred, and fear of others into my own soul; a way to not become a silent co-conspirator to the destruction and erasure of people of color.

We have the right to be angry. When my seminary classmates and professors used the word "nigger," I had the right to be angry. When other classmates told me they wished I weren't there and got up when I sat down next to them, I had the right to be angry. When non-Black people tell me my reality is not important, not relevant, not worthy of hearing, and not real, I have the right to be angry. Justifiable, expressed anger is freeing; it releases the toxic racism internalized by the gauntlet of micro- and macroaggressions hurled at Black people as we move through life.

So What If I Am an Angry Black Woman?

So what if I am an angry Black woman;
is anger only permitted to those for whom color
is painted on or fades without the sun?
Or is it an emotion only accepted from male bodies
whose lives are deemed more precious than mine?
Do you think Fannie Lou Hammer was not angry
when she was shot by the Klan for trying to register
    to vote?
Do you think Rosa Parks was not angry when she
    refused to
give her seat to a white women and was arrested for
    declaring her dignity?
Is Representative Maxine Waters not angry
every time her efforts to bring justice are dismissed?
Was Michelle Obama not angry when she was
    compared to a monkey?
So what if I am an angry Black woman;
my anger is righteous—
Born from a five-year-old girl first called "nigger"
    on the playground;

elevated by daily acts of dismissal and denigration;
the constant voices trying to convince me that I am
    less than, not fully human;
fed by systemic, cultural, and institutional white
    supremacy
that would rather imprison us than provide effective
    early education;
would rather murder us than let us be free;
would rather see us struggle for survival than fight
    for justice in the Senate.
So what if I am an angry Black woman;
it is the fuel that ignites my need for justice,
the nutrient that won't let me give up on myself,
the heart that keeps me alive and full of life.
So what if I am an angry Black woman?

White people perceive anger from Black people as a lack of control and a reason to fear or dismiss us. The Angry Black Person trope becomes, for white people, an intrinsic part of our nature that convinces them that we are capable of violence in ways that white people are inherently not. We witness it when white women pull their purses closer to themselves or roll up their windows as we pass them on the street. We witness it in the violence that police and white people use toward communities of color under the guise of "feeling threatened."

Accompanied by two members of the church's Committee on Ministry, I once visited an older member of my congregation who was expressing concern about me to other members of the congregation. After a conversation in which she said that I was working too hard, we all hugged and left. Later, she told people that I had "battered" her. Members of the congregation confronted me. Even though the committee members assured others that I had not verbally or physically assaulted the older woman, these members didn't believe it—but they believed the older white woman. It took another decade of ministry for me to undo the damage done by her careless description of my attempt to help her. After all, I was an Angry Black Woman.

Fierce, Not Angry

You say I am angry when I name your disrespect
with a loud voice and piercing eyes,
as if anger was a bad thing.
But I say no, I am not angry, I am fierce.
I am proud to the bones of who I am,
and letting you know that this Black sister
will not let you pass her by,
will not let you negate her reality, erase her existence.
My head will not bow to your dismissal.
My words will not change in the wake of your tears.
I can love you and still let you know
that you cannot break my pride,
born from generations of strong, defiant
Black women, dancing in my soul,
calling me up from the dust you would have me lie in.

I will not let the weight of your guilt diminish me,
nor the carelessness of your privilege destroy me.
I am fierce, relentlessly passionate about my worth
    and dignity;
ferociously protective of my right to thrive.
The women who own my attitude know the secret—
fierceness does not break, it roars like a lion,
soars through hurricanes, is as unmovable as a
    pyramid.
It breaks through walls and ceilings, and the dawn.
Fierceness is breathing through, not denying,
    the pain.
It is claiming the scars, not covering them up.
It's owning the anger, letting it flow out of parted
    lips,
pointed fingers, a tilted head—
not letting it possess or alter my spirit.
You say I am angry,
but you should know fierceness when you see it.

Silencing is one of the most insidious acts of white supremacy culture. White people silence Black and brown voices in many ways. They choose which BIPOC are allowed to speak, lifting up the soft-spoken—the voices they feel are less intimidating, the voices whose message "resonates." When we go off-script, are too blunt, too emotional, or too loud, they shame us and suggest that we need trauma therapy. They do not want to consider their individual culpability or examine how they contribute to the systems that perpetuate racism. And if they feel that people of color are forcing them to examine and own their part in maintaining white supremacy culture, white people squash, dismiss, and ignore.

Unitarian Universalist communities silence Black and brown people by telling us we are "pioneers" and must tread carefully. When I was in seminary, I and other students of color experienced racism at a level we didn't know how to handle. So we called our Association's headquarters and spoke with a staff member who told us that we needed to be quiet and understand that we were "sacrifices for the next generation." That same year, a minister told me that I was intimidating white students by confronting them on their racism. Many white Unitarian Universalists shame Black and brown people who, in acts of self-preservation, speak or act in ways that do not fall in line with what white people deem acceptable.

White people also silence people of color by debating with us the reality of racism. "He's not racist, he just doesn't know any better." "It wasn't racism that prevented you from getting the job, you just weren't the right fit." "She just didn't see you, that's why she stepped in front of you." Gaslit BIPOC become more and more reluctant to share our truth—the everyday experiences of living in a society that perceives us as inferior. Silence becomes both our coping mechanism and our slow death.

SILENCE

I know what Audre Lorde meant when she said
"my silence has not protected me."
Having a voice, being counted, being heard,
naming the injustice, the truth—
Well, that's breathing life, making visible the ignored,
the forgotten, the dismissed.
It is removing the shackles, breaking the ceiling of
        what is acceptable,
    breaching the surface of barriers and limitations
    put there by others
    but fully accepted by you.
For a while I thought to protect myself.
I let the hushing, the shaming, the suggestions of
        intimidation,
    the wanting to be liked, to belong . . .
    get to me.
I pretended your overtures of friendship, your
        protestations of concern,
    your disguises of support
    were not just another way to control me.
I let it be my fault, my problem.
I let you harm me—silence me, remove my power,
        dampen my life.
I've been down that path too many times,
swallowing my words, stuffing my anger,
    dying slowly, killing myself
    so that you could continue to shine.
My sisters and brothers are being wasted.

"Our children are being distorted, destroyed."[1]
All because I chose silence over living.

Due in part to white dismissal of our anger and the constant silencing of our lives and voices, Black and brown women experience depression and anxiety at greater rates than white women. Dr. Angela Neal-Barnett, professor, psychologist, and director of the Program for Research on Anxiety Disorders among African Americans at Kent State University, points out why: "Driving While Black, Shopping While Black, and everyday racial [microaggressions] are direct examples of racial trauma. The most common indirect examples are the viral videos of unarmed Black women and men being killed." How can we *not* be angry? How can we *not* experience depression?

Depression and anxiety have been my constant, if intermittent, companions since I began in the parish. Ministry is a challenging calling. We are asked to accompany people through the most devastating moments of their lives, loss after loss. We are asked to bring our best selves to situations in which others cannot or do not. We take on the role of parent, friend, authority figure, therapist, and guru. We are expected to inspire, cheerlead, draw people in, and hold up the vision

---

[1] Lorde, Audre. "The Transformation of Silence into Language and Action." First published in *Sinister Wisdom* 6 (1978) and *The Cancer Journals* (Spinsters, Ink, San Francisco, 1980).

of an earth made fair and all her people one. For ministers of
color, there is the added burden of being the representative,
example, and defender of everyone who looks like us.

Old Noise

Old Noise eatin' up my soul today.
You know—old noise, you ain't shit,
you too fat, too loud, too angry,
    too Black, not Black enough.
Noise that tells you "somehow those scars you hide
    beneath your sleeves are your fault, your doing;"
that, as you lay there, sat there, stood there, you were
      lashing yourself.
You were violating your own body, your own spirit.
You got only what you deserved.
Old noise can surprise you. Like a shadow coming
      on at sunset,
it creeps up—
when you're feeling good, owning your shit, pushing
      back your shoulders.
But in it comes, like a faint vibration, a warning of a
      seismic event.
Look out soul, look out heart, look out will to take
      one more suspicious invitation for help,
one more condescending gaze, one more fearful
      clutch of the pocketbook . . .
Don't tell me I haven't done my work.
I've been working on my Blackness, my femaleness,
my humanity my entire life.

I've named my truth, laid bare my scars, analyzed
        my part,
acknowledged the legacy.
I've burned effigies and diaries and substitutes.
I have forgiven and forgotten as much as I can.
I no longer dwell on the source of my wounds,
        I no longer think of their sources.
But like an intermittent ghost, it haunts me.
At least, it does today.

Black and brown women are forced to present a certain image in order to be accepted—another stressor on our psyches. We must be strong and stoic, stuffing down the daily trauma of racism and anger at being continually dismissed and ignored; stuffing down the anxiety of having to work harder, talk softer, and be everything to everyone in order to be seen as worthy. If we do cry, we are considered unstable or in need of trauma therapy. And yet, sometimes the sadness and pain we experience just need to be shed.

Not Surprised by Tears

As I travelled the subways and streets of New York
        City,
I noticed the tears swimming in the eyes and down
        the cheeks
of a half a dozen Black and brown women traveling
        alongside me.

I wondered at the private pain releasing itself in such a
      public space.
Anonymous in the throngs of indifferent commuters,
I struggled to lower my eyes so as not to intrude on
      their moment of release.
I am sure in a city of this size, a city known for its
      inequities, its violence,
    a city of soul-draining pace and ambition,
    a city of great wealth and deep poverty . . .
I am sure that these women were among hundreds
      shedding pain.
Having visited an embassy where crowds of poor,
      Spanish-speaking refugees
sat for hours in frustration, being told to return again
      and again with no help,
I was not surprised by these tears.
Having seen the battered Black and brown faces
left by angry boyfriends, girlfriends, and controlling
      spouses,
I was not surprised by these tears.
Having nearly tripped over the homeless and drug-
      addicted bodies
sitting and lying on cold concrete
I was not surprised by these tears.
Having experienced the unwelcome hands and groins
pressed suspiciously close to me on crowded trains,
I was not surprised by these tears.
Having visited the lonely, sick, and broken of all
      colors stacked in nursing homes
smelling of urine and antiseptic,

I was not surprised by these tears.
Knowing what it takes to survive, two or more jobs
      to make rent,
hustling to get by, selling your soul to be successful,
I was not surprised by these tears.
But I still wondered about their source and the
      possible remedies.
And so I sent a silent prayer that these tears would
      bring some peace,
that some of the frustration, pain, and trauma would
      flow away.
That breath would come more easily once the tears
      fell,
and peace and strength enough to face the next hurdle
would find its way into the spaces left by shed tears.

Questions for Discussion

1. What makes you angry? How have you been taught to deal with your anger? What messages have you received about the acceptability of anger?

2. How might you shift the way you witness and experience another person's truth-telling? How might this shift change the way you experience yourself?

3. Think of how it lands when we use other emotional adjectives to describe a person—nervous person, loving person, happy person, etc.

4. Think about a time when you were silenced or insulted for having a different perspective. How did this make you feel? When might you have done the same to others? If you are white, ask yourself if you notice when Black and brown people are being silenced. How might you interrupt this pattern of behavior?

1. What "old noise" rises for you every once in a while? List the unhelpful and unhealthy messages that repeat inside in your head. After each message, write a response that challenges that message and affirms your worth and dignity.

2. Think about other words that describe different racialized groups and how they distort the way we perceive and react to them.

3. Practice interrupting white people who center themselves and silence, dismiss, gaslight, or belittle people of color.

5

I, Too, Am Beautiful

There is beauty in darkness, brownness, and blackness—beauty in the scars and lines created by the challenge of life, beauty on and beneath the surface, beauty radiating from a diverse array of skin tones and experiences that make up our people.

The first time I read Maya Angelou's poem "Phenomenal Woman," I cried. To be able to claim my curvy, big brown body as graceful, powerful, and even phenomenal was unheard of to me. Growing up in a white-dominated society that portrayed and promoted white, thin beauty in magazines, on television, and in advertising had cultivated in me a sense of inferiority about my body. My white extended family, community, and culture constantly told me that I was Black and heavy—destined not only to die early but to be unloved and ignored.

I was confused by unflattering descriptions in books and magazines of the "ape-lipped" people of the African diaspora while at the same time white women were injecting collagen into their own lips. The white women in these magazines had straight, thin noses, whereas my short, round nose was compared to a bulldog's. I was dismayed by the negative descriptions of having "nappy" hair while white people—both men and women—were getting perms to make their hair curlier. For nearly forty years, I braided or straightened my hair, never quite liking what the mirror reflected.

My frustration with this hypocrisy and narrow image of beauty led me in 1987 to write the poem, "I, Too, Am Beautiful."

My inner spirit wrote: I have spent my life watching you, seeing your accomplishments, living the way I think you want me to. I have watched the way you move and talk. I have listened to your story and learned your history. I have sat patiently as you explained your politics, religion, and philosophy of life. I have walked with you on a journey of faith, waiting for my turn to share, explain, and lead.

I, Too, Am Beautiful

Look at me: I am Black and you are white, but I, too,
        am beautiful.
Look at my face, my hair, my clothes . . . they may be
        different
    but aren't they worthy of your gaze?
Look at my walk, the way my hips sway to the music
        in my soul,
    the way my proud neck tilts to the sun . . . yes,
        look at me.

Look at my darkness: it contains light and love,
     rebirth and growth.
Look at my pain—no, don't turn away.
Look at my experience . . . yes, listen.
I am human, I have tears and fears,
   I have laughter and joy.
Look at me and walk with me. I, too, am beautiful.

I was bewildered that my fellow classmates called my skin dirty when their older siblings and parents were spending hours on the beach and in salons trying to make their skin more like mine. I can't count the number of times white people came up to me and put their tanned arms next to mine to jealously compare "darkness."

It is the permanency of brown skin that many white people fear and see as less than human. When Broadway cast a young Black woman to play Hermione in "Harry Potter and the Cursed Child," social media lit up with racist comments about Olivier Award–winning actress Noma Dumezweni. The assumption that all book characters are white unless expressly designated "Other" is part of white supremacy culture.

To Know the Beauty of Me

I look at the brownness of my skin,
a kaleidoscope of hues shining brightly on the
     surface.

And think, "I love my color,"
although I sometimes wish I were darker,
like the deep rich shade of the mahogany tree I so
     admire.
I have always known it was not a punishment from
     an uncaring God,
but rather, the first colors of humanity—
a gift of protection from the unrelenting brightness
     of the sun.
It is the white and pink tones that are divergent,
     a hitch in our gene pool,
drawing you further from creation—
a fact yet unrealized or perhaps denied.
And still you spend hours in the harsh, unrelenting
     sun,
trying to gain a tan that is certainly not me and not
     the real you.
You use chemicals, irons, and rollers for curls that
     will never last
and that only mask the beauty of our natural
     diversity.
I have to wonder why . . .
And I think:
Fear cannot be conquered by outside manipulations
when it is the heart and soul that need transforming.
I know:
I too have tried to be you, straightening, dying, not
     knowing
what I really wanted or needed to be true—
To know the beauty of me.

During the nineteenth and early twentieth centuries, Black, brown, and white American women were subjected to social constraints that dictated how they were to behave within society. The "cult of true womanhood" or "cult of domesticity," phrases coined by historians, led to a narrow view of femininity that furthered the subjugation of all women.

The cult of womanhood operated differently for Black women than for white women. It debased enslaved Black women who were treated as disposable field hands, including pregnant women who were not exempt from working or whippings. White men further exploited enslaved Black women by sexually punishing them, which both replenished the enslaved population and terrorized them into submission.

For Black women, their status as property and servants prevented them from living up to the promoted ideals of womanhood. Because the white imagination viewed them as deviating from this established cult, they became targets for sexual discrimination, which has had enduring ramifications. Theologian Marcia Riggs notes that, "The social myths of Jezebel and Mammy continued to be used to describe and proscribe Black womanhood; the former stood as a counter-image (a woman controlled almost completely by her libido) and the latter as a Blackened version of the true woman (surrogate mistress and mother)." According to Dr. Angela Neal-Barnett, "The term Jezebel comes from the Biblical Queen who turned her husband against God. Since slavery, Black women have been sexualized in derogatory ways, often represented in [popular culture and media]."

Throughout the twentieth century, ideas of beauty and womanhood shifted only slightly for Black women. Efforts by poets like Maya Angelou and Gwendolyn Bennett to change images of Black beauty from the objectifying exotic or dismissive "Big Momma" conflicted with a culture that continues to prefer an idealized white woman to a real Black woman.

MY BEAUTIFUL BLACK SISTER

My beautiful Black sister, with your
nonconforming grace and rhythm-radiating soul.
You with the big, deep brown eyes and fierce,
    piercing gaze.
You with the long, short, curly, straight, locked
    crown,
you in all your regal baldness.
I know what lies beneath that controlled voice,
    that diminished expression.
I can see behind the veil of servant, of surrogate.
I feel the anger, the sadness, the frustration, the
    slow death
of trying to become small so others won't be
    intimidated or afraid.
I know the depression of stuffing down the roar
    of righteousness
that claims our humanity, our value, our right to
    name the truth.

I see your goddess, your divine love,
the depth of your Black brilliance.
I hope someday you will too. See the
years of survival not as a test, but a testimony
to a stubborn love born from generations of strong
    Black sisters—
mothers who refused to give up, grandmothers who
    passed down
more than recipes of arroz con pollo, tandoori, and
    fried chicken. Sisters
and aunts who held one another up, reached out a
    hand,
shook us when we needed to wake up.
My beautiful Black sisters with your
doubt and your brokenness and your dusty knees . . .
You are loved.

I have spent most of my life admiring the beauty and depth of Black and brown women. I feel a connection that draws me to them and a pride that strengthens my own. The passion and pain, the joy and laughter, and the years of persevering and pushing Sisyphus's stone only to have it roll back over us again and again have only intensified my awe of all that is held in these beautiful bodies.

Brown Sister

I watch my brown sister walk down the street.
It's not just her skin and hair and eye that speak of
      her brownness;
her whole being radiates a narrative shared only by
      those of dark hues.
She could be 30 or perhaps 60; her smooth face
      denies her age.
I notice the slight smile that holds a secret—
    the feel of the wind, the scent of her lover, the
      relief of another day done.
Her head is held high from practice, from pride,
      from strength,
denying the generations of bending and bowing.
Rhythm from music I cannot hear moves her hips,
beautiful, sexy, inviting movement, calling for me
      to join her.
I know that drum. The one that traveled with us
      over oceans and deserts,
across the border, along the plains, out from the woods.
It is the beat of celebration, of joy, of anger, of war.
It is the imitation of the heart outside the chest
      pounding to life.
My sister does not pause, as there is no time—
life does not take a break
    for the ones whose survival resides in continuous
      motion.
There are children at home, or perhaps that lover.
      Dinner to make,
    or maybe only more emptiness to avoid.

But for that moment, as my admiring gaze takes in
        her beautiful brownness
I find myself in love with our oneness. In love with
        the history we share,
the barriers we have climbed, the violence and
        degradation we have survived.
I am in love with the layers contained in our color
        and give thanks.

QUESTIONS FOR DISCUSSION

1. From who or what did you learn what you consider beautiful? Think about how those ideals might be racialized in subtle and overt ways.

2. How might the beauty of someone's heart and soul redefine your understanding of their physical beauty?

3. How do you transmit your ideals of beauty to others?

1. Create a collage that portrays a large range of beauty, and write about why you chose those images.

2. Explore the history of whitewashed roles, where white people play characters of color in movies and on television (for example, Emma Stone as Allison Ng in *Aloha* or Donna Reed as Sacajawea in *The Far Horizons*). Write an essay about why whitewashing was once widely acceptable in Hollywood, but a Black or brown actor portraying a character viewed as white was met with mainstream resistance.

3. In London, a new trend called "blind casting" has emerged, where actors are picked for roles with no regard to their race, ethnicity, gender, or body type. List the ways in which this trend might shift entertainment industry culture in the United States.

6

I Am Not Your Homegirl

One day I walked into the sanctuary of a majority-white congregation, looking around for a direction to head. Small groups of people milled about, some wearing name tags and preparing the room for service, others laughing or talking seriously in private conversations. I wondered if they would notice me and rush over or pretend I wasn't there. Where should I go? Whom should I interrupt? I stood for what felt like a long time, waiting to be acknowledged and greeted, but my presence went unmarked. I began to explore the room, walking around looking at the pictures and banners, symbols and candles, the markings of a life of faith. Nothing on the walls suggested that I was welcome there.

I headed to the membership table, where a volunteer was speaking with another visitor, a smartly dressed white woman with grey hair. The volunteer focused solely on the person in front of her. After ten minutes, I started to wonder about their aggressive concentration and efforts to not acknowledge me.

Finally I walked away, ready to leave. But I couldn't. I was the guest speaker that day and needed to find someone who would tell me where to be. Finally, a white minister saw me. He smiled, came down the center aisle, and greeted me, "What's up, homegirl?" he asked. And I stopped wondering.

White society's relationships with Black and brown people have been mixed. A few white-led organizations have been able to attract and be in covenantal relationships with communities of color through intention, commitment, humility, and curiosity. Others have stumbled again and again to center the reality of the diversity, joy, pain, and gifts of people of color. Still others have completely denied us our full humanity and worth, as their inner fears and stereotypes dictate their relationships with Black and brown people.

While the United States often reduces the diversity of its people to the proverbial "melting pot," I remember my initial surprise and sympathy for young white people I would see in Boston trying to consume African, Asian, Indigenous, and Latinx cultures through dreadlocked hair, imitating the walking and speech patterns of urban Black communities, and wearing saris and dashikis, all to proclaim their coolness. Members of my faith community have used pieces, parts, and whole rituals, music, writings, and rites from BIPOC communities without the appropriate context, care, or thought about how their cultural appropriation diminishes and profits from Black and brown cultures.

White institutions and companies also appropriate images of people of color for their websites and brochures as examples of their "welcoming and affirming" culture. This tokenization of BIPOC only further silences and demeans us by transforming us into objects, not real people with depth and feelings.

However, the white desire to take pieces of cultures of color does not translate into a deeper engagement with the communities from which they are appropriating. When a person of color goes off-script—if their truth is too painful or pointed for white people to receive—they are not invited back, or are isolated and pushed aside. Our accomplishments are only acknowledged if they comply with white people's expectations of us or improve their status with other white people.

I AM STRONG, I AM FIERCE, I AM INTELLIGENT,
I AM . . .

I am not the Black woman you want me to be,
quiet and contained, accepting of all your "mistakes,"
your faux pas, your hurtful words and actions.
I am strong, I am fierce, I am intelligent, I am . . .

She is not the Indian woman you think she is,
cowed by her husband
sitting obediently, nodding
in acceptance of your dismissal.
I am strong, I am fierce, I am intelligent, I am . . .

She is not the Asian woman you expect her to be,
meek and silent, agreeing with your exceptionalism,
accepting your eroticizing, taking the verbal punches
    with grace.
I am strong, I am fierce, I am intelligent, I am . . .

She is not the Latina woman your stereotypes
    demand,
a childbearing, hot-tempered maid,
who doesn't understand your mocking words,
your dismissing looks, your sexualized scan.
I am strong, I am fierce, I am intelligent, I am . . .

She is not the Indigenous woman you portray her as,
conflating hundreds of tribes, thousands of peoples.
She is not the vessel of your atonement,
the token you take out to prove your connection to
    the earth.
I am strong, I am fierce, I am intelligent, I am . . .

I will not be silenced by your dismissal,
cowed by your bullying, shamed by the scars
you add to my soul.
I will not be stopped by your fear or hatred.
Your self-loathing is not mine. Your crimes are not
    mine.
No lash of tongue or hand will strip me of my
    dignity,
for I am strong, I am fierce, I am intelligent,
    I am . . . me!

White people so often fail to see beyond skin color. I have been unable to count the number of times I have been called by another Black woman's name. At an annual UUA meeting in Nashville, Tennessee, a white woman came up to me and congratulated me on a wonderful worship service and workshop; I knew immediately that she had confused me with Rev. Alma Faith Crawford. At the time, there were fewer than ten ordained and fellowship Black women in my faith tradition, and we all knew each other. I explained to the white woman that I wasn't Alma; she turned bright red and started to walk away. But I stopped her, introduced myself, and invited her to look at me. To see who I was. I wasn't angry at her, as she had never met me and we were not in relationship.

However, over the years, the number of colleagues and lay people who called me by another Black woman's name grew, as did my frustration. Their response was frequently apologetic, but just as often, my correction was met with annoyance or irritation.

The most hurtful example of these microaggressions took place at the church my adoptive father and stepmother attended. My dad, the president and a member of the choir, had been there for more than a decade, and I had preached there before. I was scheduled as a guest speaker; when I arrived, I was handed an order of service with my name below a photo of Rev. Sophia Betancourt. I lifted up the picture in the middle of the service and said, "This is not me. This is the Rev. Sophia Betancourt." Everyone laughed—except me.

This inappropriate laughter, to divert attention from the harm that was done, or to diminish the feelings of the person of color who has just been dismissed, is part of the language of racism.

See Me!

Why do you not see me?
My dark skin does not blur the shape of my eyes,
      the curve of my face,
the fullness of my lips.
Can you not read my crinkled brow and understand
      your mistake?
You call the spirit of another person out from me,
ignoring your experience with her, your history
      with her,
your opinion of her;
sending my essence shuffling back deep inside—
dismissed as unworthy of your attention.
You do not want me or my gifts.
You are reaching for another's life.
Who I am fades into nothingness.
All I've accomplished erased in one word.
"Kristen," I say. "My name is Kristen."

The coded and direct language that white people often use not only denies their ties to us but also demeans us. At an annual gathering of my faith tradition, my husband was supervising our African American and Indian godsons as they played outside the convention center. An older couple who had just been nearly run down by two exuberant three-year-olds told my husband to "keep his little monkeys in line." This racist imagery is both vile and widespread. Just over a decade earlier, an MCI commercial depicted a number of countries with smiling white people wearing cultural attire; for the entire continent of Africa, the advertisers used a monkey to represent the African people.

As a result of racist language and imagery, many BIPOC have felt betrayed, traumatized, and excluded. We are suspicious of any white assertion that "Black Lives Matter" and are hurt when white people fail to appreciate the full reality of our existence. And because white people continue to cause harm to people of color in our families, friendship circles, communities, and nation; because they lack the imagination needed to dismantle white supremacist culture, their building and maintaining relationships with us remains a challenge.

Many faith communities, including my own, have made tremendous strides in our justice work. They are following the lead of marginalized communities, becoming allies where possible, and showing up when asked. However, there are generations of mistrust to cross and continued white supremacist thinking to shed before authentic relationships can grow and survive. As I said nearly twenty years ago in my sermon, "Bridges Go Both Ways," "the first things we so often fail to do is building bridges that go both ways, bridges of friendship, bridges of relationships, of trust and honesty, [of accountability and reconciliation]. This is what is so hard—BIPOC and white people learning to trust one another, be with one another, truly care for and be committed to one another."

It Begins With . . .

It begins with knowing
your biases, your stereotypes,
your assumptions, your judgments
and how to set them aside and receive the person
who is in front of you, not the one you think you
    know.
It begins with owning
your power and privilege,
your position and your comfort
and being willing to let it go.
It begins with truly looking at one another,
noticing that not all Black and brown people look
    alike,
are alike, believe alike, experience, or react alike.
It begins with reaching out,
Making the first move,
Offering the first invitation for coffee or tea,
or a walk in the park, or a trip to a museum.
It begins with hello—
not a touching of hair or bodies,
just hello.

It begins with curiosity
about our full lives,
not about the hard experiences,
not if Black and brown skin burns in the sun,
not about dreadlocks, or braids, or straight black hair.
It begins with listening,
not constantly centering yourselves,
but to whatever is shared, whatever is believed,
whatever is meaningful, whatever might connect.
It begins with attention
to your words, your language, your expressions
and the impact they have,
without dismissing or belittling.
It begins with understanding,
not making judgments about Christian, Buddhist,
Hindu, Humanist, or Earth-centered faith.
Understanding that there are many ways to believe,
all valid, all restorative, all equal.
It begins with accompaniment—following, not
    leading,
learning, not teaching, supporting, not just taking.
It begins with commitment
to stay with each other through the discomfort and
    anger,
to bridge the barriers, to build trust.
It begins with accepting the joy and the challenges,
the quirky or protective actions,
the need for space where you may not be able to
    follow,
the need for distance that you may not be able to
    bridge.

It begins with believing
the experiences so foreign from your own:
the daily fights for dignity,
the trauma of a life of surviving the gauntlet of hate
    and ignorance,
the mixture of laughter and tears, passion and
    sorrow.
It begins—whether a relationship, a friendship, or a
    partnership—
it begins with you.

QUESTIONS FOR DISCUSSION

1. What was your earliest encounter with a culture different from your own? What did you appreciate about that culture?

2. Why does the context of when, why, and by whom a ritual was created matter?

3. In what ways have white people appropriated Black and brown cultures?

4. Do you know the expression "All Black people look alike"? How does this stereotype operate in our society?

Exercises

1. List some appropriate ways to show appreciation for other cultures.

2. Explore rituals from your own cultures and examine their context.

3. Create a ritual, prayer, or rite that speaks to your current context and culture.

4. White readers: when you misname a person of color, what can you do to handle it gracefully instead of getting irritated or turning away in embarrassment?

5. How can you move your practice of antiracism from the realm of thoughts and ideas into concrete actions?

7

Identity Politics and Oppressive Language

In recent years, new language has arisen in an effort to deflect the hurt and anger people of color experience in faith communities. As Black and brown people have begun to assert our power and demand to move from margin to center, white people have used coded language to silence and demean us. Phrases and words such as "identity politics," "assume goodwill," "a common humanity," and "safetyism" have emerged under the guise of rationality to point the criticism back at Black and brown communities for naming anti-Blackness and white supremacy and for claiming our worth and rights as human beings. This coded language tries to silence the real harm many white people continue to do through thoughtlessness, ignorance, and the conscious and unconscious desire to maintain their superiority in the world.

The language of "identity politics" is often thrown at people of color when we name our desire to enjoy the same privileges and respect afforded to white people. Proponents of this accusation claim that the issues and concerns of Black and brown people are specific only to us—that we prioritize our needs above the needs of a "common humanity."

The racism embedded in this language has many implications: that all members of an ethnic or racial group hold the same political lens and identities, that people of color are a monolith, and that the concerns of Black and brown people do not intersect with the concerns or interests of white people.

The *Stanford Encyclopedia of Philosophy* defines identity politics as "a wide range of political activity and theorizing found in the shared experiences of injustice of members of certain social groups. Rather than organizing solely around belief systems, programmatic manifestos or party affiliation, identity political formations typically aim to secure the political freedom of a specific constituency marginalized within its larger context. Members of the constituency assert or reclaim ways of understanding their distinctiveness that challenge dominant oppressive characterizations, with the goal of greater self-determination."

The assumption underlying the dismissal of "identity politics" is that identity should not be a factor in political engagement. This misunderstanding ignores the fact that BIPOC have joined together across identities to raise issues that affect not only their individual lives and communities but the lives of all marginalized people. The Poor People's Campaign and immigration justice movements have united the concerns of people with multiple racial and cultural identities. Lack of equal access to education and employment opportunities, the biases in the criminal justice system, housing and food insecurity, and the systematic disenfranchisement of incarcerated, poor, elderly, and Black and brown people are issues that span many demographics.

Of the twenty-two transgender women murdered in 2019, nineteen were Black. Of the 996 men shot by the police in 2018, 209 were Black, 148 were Latinx, and 240 were considered "other" or "race unknown." While Indigenous men are often left out of such statistics or lumped under "other," new research from Rutgers University, Washington University in St. Louis, and the University of Michigan shows that police are even more likely to murder Indigenous men than Latinx men. Furthermore, in 2017 the Henry J. Kaiser Family Foundation reported that while eight percent of people living in poverty were white, twenty-two percent were Indigenous Alaskan Native; twenty percent, Black; sixteen percent, Latinx; and nine percent, Asian, Native Hawaiian, and Pacific Islander. Communities of color have long recognized the intersectionality of multiple oppressions and continue to organize across race, religion, ethnicity, immigration, class, and climate.

At the Intersections of America

At the intersections of America,
where race and ethnicity, economics and ability,
gender and sexual orientation meet,
I find my center . . .
Next to my friend who smiles broadly as she claims
    her position,
a poor Black Lesbian
and still proud, still radiating beauty,
still striving to rise and embracing love . . .

Next to my friend who is disabled,
an immigrant from Nicaragua,
a self-proclaimed Black Latinx who speaks in her
    own vernacular.
A woman who loves other women, a triple threat,
and although in tremendous pain, rises each day,
to the challenges and joys of motherhood,
to the barriers and bridges of culture and race,
to the call of God and community,
with grace and openness, honesty and humility . . .

Next to my friend who identifies as Wampanoag
    and Black,
living in subsidized housing, raising three boys
    alone
in a world that fears who she has given birth to,
denigrates the old gods that keep her steady,
and pollutes the land she describes as the marrow
    of her bones.
And even though tears of sorrow and frustration fall,

born of the consistent dismissal and silencing
from those who are squatters on land they took
    from her ancestors,
from those who survived by her people's graces,
from those who fail to see the well of intellect and
    beauty . . .

Next to these women and many others,
I, a Black Jewish woman, a bridge builder,
    a broken heart,
find my center, with their powerful pride, their
    powerful spirits,
their powerful message—
At the intersections of America, you will find the
    soul of America.
It is messy and loud, silent and fierce,
complicated and joyous, tender and bruised.
It is music and dancing, food and chosen family.
It is deep disagreement and deep appreciation.
It is multiple generations of stories and histories,
lessons and traditions, innovation and creativity.
At the intersections of America,
you will find our salvation.

A few years ago, I was asked to lead a worship service with
a colleague at a meeting of ministers and religious educators.
I introduced a ritual where people would pick up pebbles,
symbolizing the joys and sorrows we carry around with us, and
put them into a bowl of water, representing our community

of hope and compassion. I invited a relatively new colleague to add additional stones for people who were there, for the world we live in, for the earth that nurtures and nourishes us, and for all those joys and sorrows too scary or too private to lift up at that time. As I was naming the additional pebbles, my colleague interrupted me and closed out the ritual. Was she tired of adding pebbles after only two? Did she think I didn't know how to end a ritual? Would she have done the same to a white colleague? When I named her inappropriate behavior, other colleagues told me to "assume goodwill."

"Assume goodwill" is language used by white people that burdens BIPOC rather than themselves to consider the impact of their words and actions. It implies that, no matter what happens, the person of color is the one responsible for ending the conflict. There is no language for "assume that a person who says they are hurt is hurt."

The phrase "assume goodwill" is often added to the covenants we create in our congregations, our minister's groups, and our larger efforts at organizing community. Over the nearly fifty years I have been a Unitarian Universalist, I have come to the conclusion that those with privilege routinely use it to excuse their lack of attention to what they say and do to people with marginalized identities. When we name the hurt that has been caused, we become the problem. If we had only assumed goodwill, then we would not feel harmed, or would recognize our feelings as unreasonable—the result of being too sensitive or projecting our feelings onto other people. The language of "assuming goodwill" distorts our reality and blames people of color who are hurt by the words and actions of their white companions in faith.

Assume Goodwill

How do I assume goodwill when you fail to notice who I am as you ask me to plunge your overflowing toilets, to park your car, to carry your luggage? How do I assume goodwill when you interrupt me again and again or ignore my requests for help? How do I assume goodwill when you call me out of my name and get angry when I insist who I really am? How do I assume goodwill when you let people of your race step in front of me as if I were invisible, when you fill the glasses of white people first even when they are not thirsty? How do I assume goodwill when you repeatedly "forget" to return my calls?

How do I assume goodwill when you call my godsons "little monkeys," when you say I am an exception, when you say, "Black people are not intelligent enough to lead our faith," when you get up when I sit down next to you? How can I assume goodwill when you use poetic license to excuse your use of "nigger" and other racial slurs? How can I assume goodwill when you refuse to witness the pain, the hurt, the erasure of who I am that you contribute to with your thoughtlessness and lack of intention?

You have not consistently shown goodwill when you suggest I was an affirmative action hire, a quota filler, a balm for white guilt. You have failed to demonstrate goodwill when you judge me by my "accent" and my different approaches to faith, community, love, and justice. Is asking me if I write my own sermons "goodwill"? Is assuming I know what all my kindred of color are thinking and experiencing "goodwill"?

Is interrupting my leadership of worship because you believe you know how to do it better "goodwill"? Is denigrating my efforts to make change so that all may participate in the beloved community "goodwill"?

I cannot assume anything as such when you feel it is your right to touch me without asking. I cannot assume anything when you allow no room for my humanity, my brokenness, my joy, my diverse ways of seeing the world. I cannot assume anything when you welcome me into your spaces with suspicion and fear. I will assume nothing . . . until you stop assuming about me.

A member of my congregation offered a wonderful metaphor for Unitarian Universalism: a light covered in a shade with a multitude of holes where light shines through in different angles, at different intensities, and refracting different colors. Depending on the size of the holes and your position in relation to the lampshade, you might experience different kinds of radiance. This has always been a more helpful image than the melting pot, tossed salad, or other smorgasbord analogies used to describe our theological, racial, ethnic, gender, class, sexual, physical, cognitive, and emotional diversity. It emphasizes the oneness of our source while providing insight into why each of us remains unique and how our experiences can seem so divergent. Depending on the angle of our perception and the amount of shadow and color we receive, we can change our experience of the source and others' experience of our radiance. And yet we still remain many of one.

I prefer this image to the language of "a common humanity," the assertion that our experiences as human beings, particularly those suffering, are shared by most people, and that if we can recognize that our individual experiences and needs are shared by all of humanity then we will no longer feel alone and develop a greater compassion for all. Albert Einstein asserted, "A human being is a part of the whole called by us 'universe,' a part limited in time and space. He experiences himself, his thoughts and feelings as something separated from the rest, a kind of optical delusion of his consciousness. This delusion is a kind of prison for us, restricting us to our personal desires and to affection for a few persons nearest to us. Our task must be to free ourselves from this prison by widening our circle of compassion to embrace all living creatures and the whole of nature in its beauty."

However, this language assumes that our common humanity is white and that therefore white concerns and interests should be the supreme focus. It suggests that since suffering itself is universal, focusing on the specifics of who experiences more "imprisons" us. This approach is beneficial primarily to the privileged, implying that marginalized people should have compassion for the people who cause their suffering. It lays the responsibility at the feet of the marginalized and not where it belongs—with those who cause lifelong, generational, and often debilitating harm to others. Yes, we all suffer. We all grieve. We all experience loss, sadness, and heartache. However, not all of us have our reality denied. Not all of us are demeaned, dismissed, and verbally and physical assaulted because of our identities. Not all of us fear being murdered by the very people we pay to protect us. Not all of us live in a world where our humanity is judged by our vernacular, our gender, our skin color, our physical and cognitive abilities, or who we love.

For example, white society assumes that people of color are less than fully human and are here to serve them. Once, while attending an annual Unitarian Universalist meeting in Phoenix, Arizona, my husband and I—who wore badges noting we were part of the convention—were asked to plunge the toilets that were overflowing in the convention center's bathroom. When we informed our fellow conventioneers that we were part of their group, the white couple simply stood there looking at us until we turned away and left.

The framework of "a common humanity" is problematic because it is a fantasy based on homogeny and does not reflect the wildly different realities experienced by people and groups. We may be from the same source, but we are each different beams of light radiating through pinholes of various sizes and shapes that change how we perceive ourselves and others. The variations in shade and intensity make catching glimpses of our oneness so challenging that the idea of "a common humanity" is a dream that must be deferred.

A Different Dream

"I have a dream," said Martin Luther King Jr.,
but that dream has not come to pass.
"We are all God's children," says the bible,
but to a world who paints our Lord white,
it is clear who are his favorites.
So we continue to march in protest
against a system not designed for us,
to stand in vigil once again as another Black or
    brown life
is senselessly taken by those who cannot see a
    common humanity.
Do we continue to push ahead, stuffing down the
    pain and humiliation,
trying to prove we are equality qualified, equally
    worthy, equally deserving?
I too went to college, received honors, and graduated
    with a debt
that will last my nieces' and nephews' lifetimes.
I too pay taxes, wondering why I pay for services
    often denied to me,

safety nets that may not be available for my old age.
I too have a dream,
but unlike the honorable Rev. Dr. King,
I know it is not the little children of God
who need to hold hands and let freedom ring.
My dream is that one day the world will stop trying
   to merge us into one.
I do not want to become lost in the melting pot of
   uniformity.
I am not suggesting segregation or separatism—rather
   true pluralism.
Would you have us erase the soul of the blues or the
   essence of rock?
Where would we be without rice and beans, meat and
   potatoes, jambalaya and baklava?
Where would we be without the taiko drums of Japan,
the steel drums of Trinidad and Tobago, or the djembe
   drums of West Africa?
Where would we be without variety or spice, whether
   of crayons or of cars?

We are not a democracy without Muhammad,
   Brahma, Allah, and God.
We are not a land of freedom when differences are
   merely tolerated.
We cannot be a United States until diversity is
   respected,
admired, blessed, and honored.
This here is my dream.
Is it not easier to learn to appreciate,
instead of ignoring or eliminating,

those differences we know so little of and therefore
   fear?
I dream a beloved community of multicultural
   splendor,
Where everyone is centered and all are supreme.
I dream of a world where we feed one another
and live in cooperation with the earth.
I dream of a Universe where every color of light shines
against the beautiful dark that embraces us all.

Questions for Discussion

1. Which multiple identities do you hold, and how do they impact your experience of the world and relationships to other people?

2. Name some of the issues that are unique to your identities. Can you recognize intersections with the identities of other people?

3. What metaphor or story do you use to balance our oneness and our diversity?

4. What are the strengths and challenges of individuality? Of communal identity?

EXERCISES

1. Come up with a story, poem, or picture that depicts the unity in diversity.

2. Make a list of all the social justice issues that you are passionate about. Under each one, list the different ways they intersect with other justice issues.

3. Think about your dreams for the United States or for humanity in general. List the necessary benchmarks needed to attain that dream.

8

Quotas, Affirmative Action, and Political Correctness

I will never forget a visit by the Ministerial Fellowship Committee, the credentialing body of the Unitarian Universalist Association, during the spring of my first year in seminary. One of my white classmates asked a representative what the "quota" was for granting fellowship to candidates of color. At the time, Meadville Lombard Theological School had the largest number of students of color attending in its history; there were about eight of us. Racial tensions were high as we BIPOC students made known our voices, faith, opinions, and displeasure about the racism we were experiencing in seminary.

Quotas began as an affirmative action effort to address racial and gender discrimination and underrepresentation of BIPOC and women in business and higher education. Its intention was to place equally qualified women and people of color in positions from which they were historically shut out, enabling them to be promoted into positions historically dominated by white men. Businesses seeking government contracts had to prove they had a certain percentage of women and "minorities" working for them. State-run academic institutions were required to review the number of female students and people with marginalized identities entering and graduating as benchmarks of progress.

In the early 1990s, I attended an antiracism workshop led by UU minister Rev. Dr. William Jones, a professor of religion at Florida State University. He described the effects of slavery and Jim Crow on Black people as like having your leg tied behind your back for twenty years. Even once the rope is untied, the muscles will be atrophied. Learning to simply hold your weight would be challenging. Imagine then, he explained, that life is like a track field, with Black people and white people lined up to race. How long would it take for the Black person, who is disadvantaged from the start, to catch up? Even if there were no barriers—equal access to resources, education, and employment; a just criminal justice system; equal advancement and pay; and virtually no discrimination— even then, the likelihood that the Black person could catch up is doubtful. But these barriers are real and do exist. The intergenerational effects of slavery, Jim Crow, and systemic racism have kept many BIPOC behind as we seek to untie the vestiges of white supremacy.

Whether from a fear of scarcity or a basic fear of people of color, some white people perceive quota systems as "reverse discrimination." Others use it as a weapon to demean the qualifications of people they deem "affirmative action hires" or "quota fillers."

Once during seminary, some white students told a couple of us women of color that we were only there because of affirmative action. Although I was awarded Dean's Scholar and was one of only two classmates to receive a doctorate, there was still never enough proof of our accomplishments for white people to accept that we deserved to be there. At an antiracism training I attended in 1994, one minister, in response to the concern that there weren't enough people of color in Unitarian Universalism, exclaimed "But Black people aren't intelligent enough to be Unitarian Universalists!" This was after a 1989 Commission on Appraisal study found that, as Mark Morrison-Reed writes in *Black Pioneers in a White Denomination*, "income and educational levels among Black Unitarian Universalists are slightly higher than average" among Unitarian Universalists—who are already the most highly educated and highest income religious denomination in the US.

What Your Degrees Have Not Taught You

Your degree has not taught you true equality:
that we are each precious children of one universe.
That the blood in my veins is as blue as yours.
That what you have doesn't make you better
than those that have not.
That you deserve no more nor no less than others.
Your degree has not taught you real acceptance—

that embracing difference will only make you stronger;
that diversity draws you deeper into life,
deeper into yourself and all you have to offer.
Your degree has not taught you how to look at your
    mistakes
and laugh in your belly at the humanity unveiled,
nor to forgive and move on from the unattainable
    perfection
that will always elude you.
Your degree has not taught you to feel the heartbeat
    of the earth,
to feel the trees calling and the wind teasing and the
    water roaring;
nor how to be transformed in a sunbeam and soar to
    the heavens.
Your degree has not taught you how to love universally,
to see beyond the masks others wear
into the hearts that ache and want and need just as
    you do.
Your degree did not teach you to accept the death
    we all come to
and find rest in the grace of the warm, dark universe
and find yourself a star among the planets.

When I was a child, I was taught to be twice as smart,
work twice as hard, and do twice as well as the white kids if I
wanted to succeed. I saw how the white kids received more
attention and praise for the same work . . . and I learned. I

learned from their ostracism to not be too intimidating. I learned from their taunts to not stand out. I learned from their violence to not strike back but instead to use my silence and my words to make my mark. I learned to survive. Survival might not be a subject in any university's doctoral program, but I have a PhD in survival. I am still alive and so it has been very useful.

When I was young, I learned that to accept white people's stereotypes would only wither my soul. So I found my voice and named injustices. I marched for equality, rallied for freedom, protested oppression, and pushed back when pushed on. I learned the legends of our prophets—the Kings and the Carmichaels, the Angelous and the Hamers, the X's and the Shakurs, and the Davises and the Morrisons. And I learned resistance. I learned to resist being just one of the crowd, doing as others expected and pretending that nothing was wrong. I am still resisting.

As an adult, I have learned that to survive and resist is not enough. That my spirit needs to heal, soar, and find acceptance. And so I am learning to thrive. I am learning to embrace all of who I am, to dance out the disappointments, to sing the sorrows into the wind, and to throw off the shame that is not mine to carry. I have learned that thriving is not just about connecting with joy but about embracing the full range of life's emotions. To thrive is to experience ecstasy from the roots of my hair through the ends of my toes. It is to sob with abandon and love myself without limit. It is to dive into the brokenness that is our world and find the hope and healing, and to feed as many hungry souls as I can.

According to Cynthia Roper of *Encyclopedia Britannica*, political correctness is a "term used to refer to language that seems intended to give the least amount of offense, especially when describing groups identified by external markers such as race, gender, culture, or sexual orientation." Political correctness was first used after the 1917 Russian Revolution in Marxist-Leninist circles to describe "adherence to the policies and principles of the Communist Party of the Soviet Union." In the 1970s and 80s, liberal politicians coopted the term to poke fun at what they considered the extreme views of the far left. The term reemerged in the 1990s with conservatives who used it to characterize the rise of liberalism on university and college campuses.

We liberal religionists have had an uneasy relationship with political correctness. While we have embraced individual freedom of belief, the responsible search for truth and meaning, and freedom of the pew and pulpit to speak our individual truths, we have also hurt and traumatized many by misnaming, excluding, and stereotyping. In our efforts to be truly inclusive, we are often charged with appealing to the lowest common denominator and stifling freedom of speech. While healthy debate has always been a cornerstone of Unitarian Universalism, when it comes to racism, sexism, homophobia, heterosexism, transphobia, classism, and ableism, we have leaned toward intolerant views that question, challenge, or deny the need for care and caution when discussing marginalized people.

As a Black woman who is always caught off guard when someone calls me "African American," a term I have never used to describe myself, I understand the power and importance of self-naming. I also recognize the exclusion, hurt, and invisibility I have felt when others weren't willing to simply ask me what I preferred to be called. But it wasn't until the debate around ableist language in Unitarian Universalist hymns that I truly came face-to-face with my own privilege and my ability to dismiss the concerns of other marginalized people. As I wrestled with the request to not sing "Standing on the Side of Love" because it implies that only those who are physically able to stand can be on the side of love, I felt the discomfort and annoyance of having to stretch myself yet again. And then it hit me: this was not about adhering to some principle or policy, but a request for inclusion, a request to be acknowledged as full human beings and as participants in our faith. It was an issue of covenant and of honoring the inherent worth and dignity of every person.

I AM A BLACK WOMAN

You do not get to choose who I am,
    what I think, how I feel.
You do not get to label my lived experiences,
    my joy, my pain, how I survived.

I am a Black Woman,
    a descendant from the likes of *La Amistad*
    born in the fever of civil rights passions and hope.
I flouted the "colorblindness" of the times
    and named my Blackness to all who refused to see.
I am a descendant of generations of rabbis,
    survivors of Poland's part in the Holocaust,
    following the treads of many men
    more devout and confident than I.
I am a child of the woods, of pine and birch and oak
      trees,
    with the smell of fertile earth always lingering in
      my nostrils.
I am cisgender, heterosexual, abled;
    I get a pass for the woman I am,
privileged by the cohesion of biology and identity
    that clings to a binary, uncomplicated and
      controlled;
    privileged by the oppressive heterosexual norms,
    that fail to acknowledge the range of sexuality;
    privileged by the ableist world I inhabit
    that denies the diversity of bodies, minds, and
      souls,
    the diversity of full humanity.
Call me by my name, my choice, my decision
    and I will do the same for you.
I am a Black Woman,
    one of the survivors of this messy, fearful,
      angry world,
    hoping one day to thrive.

Questions for Discussion

1. What steps have you taken to support people of color in your congregation?

2. For white readers, have you ever noticed yourself becoming uncomfortable as more BIPOC join the congregation? What can you do to work through that discomfort?

3. What would you have to change in order to be truly welcoming to BIPOC?

4. In what ways are you being asked to stretch your understanding of welcome and acceptance? What must you tear down—traditions and customs, lack of knowledge of other cultures, feeling "drowned out" or "taken over"—to reach this level of understanding?

5. Have you ever had to ask people to stretch to truly welcome you—spiritually, culturally, economically, physically, or emotionally?

1. White readers: Think about all the times in your life that you were offered an opportunity and what helped you get that offer, such as the school you attended, a family connection, a previous job, easy transportation, a scholarship, or family financial support.

2. Readers of color: Think about when you were denied an opportunity and what barriers prevented you from getting that offer. When were you able to overcome these barriers and how?

9

The Greatest Trick: Internalized Oppression

THE GREATEST TRICK

How did you manage to convince so many of us
    that we were less than?
How did you persuade us
    that our skin was not beautiful, vibrant, healthy,
        clean?
How did you fool us into believing
    that we were not intelligent, not resourceful, not
        powerful?
How did you make us believe our lives did not matter
    as much as yours?
Was it the names you called us: monkey, nigger,
        savage, boy, girl, thug?
Was it the violence you perpetrated upon us;
    the chains, the whips, the nooses, the knees on
        our throats, the bullets in our chests?
Was it the poverty and environmental degradation
        you trapped us in?
    In towers of despair, on land poisoned by your
        greed.

Was it the looting of our music, our culture, our
     bodies?
  Taking what you thought was the best of us,
  stealing what you could, claiming it to be yours.
Was it the twisting of our experiences
  and claiming that our lived reality wasn't real?
Was it the blame you laid on us for what you—for
     centuries—inflicted on us?
We know your game now, your strategy to keep us
     in our place.
We see into your hearts, into the twisted logic of
     your fear,
and invite you to tear down your illusions and
     self-perpetuating lies.
For we will continue to remove the masks that you
     placed and the chains you hung on us.
We will no longer bow in the dirt for the scraps of
     humanity you offer.
We own who we are, beautiful, powerful, intelligent,
     worthy—
  fully human and completely precious.

Throughout this book, I have attempted both to present new imagery of blackness and darkness for white people and people of color to ponder and to name the harm that white culture has perpetrated on Black and brown communities. Internalized oppression is the absorption of prejudices, stereotypes, inferiority, and even self-hatred that white supremacy culture beats into Black and brown people and communities.

We have witnessed internalized oppression in celebrities such as Michael Jackson and Lil' Kim who have lightened their skin, thinned their noses and lips, or erased their bone structure. It appears in the constant use of chemicals to straighten our hair and the preference for weaves and wigs over our natural curls and braids. It's the shame many of us feel whenever a Black or brown person commits a crime, as if they represent the entire community. It's the blaming of Black youth and young adults for the generational poverty they find themselves trapped in and the violence they inflict upon one another. Internalized oppression rears its ugly head when we cringe at the way some of our people speak or tease those of us from the country, from the city, or from less educated families. Internalized oppression is what causes us to wear colored contacts, to judge each other on our proximity to whiteness, or when we call people "Oreo," "High Yellow," or "Redbone." It entices us to create universal standards of Blackness that all Black people must follow.

Internalized oppression is a trick to keep Black and brown people down and divided, not thriving and creating our own inclusive, united, diverse communities.

NOW IS OUR TIME TO THRIVE

Where the Mississippi River and the Gulf of Mexico intersect,
the rulers of Spain, Portugal, France, and England claimed their manifest destiny, their superiority,

their right to own, to tear apart, to break down
generations of lives, leaving specters of souls
clinging to failed survival and unfulfilled hopes.
On the banks of New Orleans, the upheaval of the
    Middle Passage
gave way to further trauma,
not just in the form of rape and castration, whips
    and chains.
The greatest trick was to convince a people
of their inherent unworthiness, their permanent
    status of supplicant.
The greatest trick was the inculcation of self-hatred,
    self-denial,
self-limiting fear, toxic rage, and hopelessness.
The greatest trick was to sell the afterlife as an
    exchange
for freedom and dignity.
We demand today an end to this bargain we did
    not negotiate.
An end to participating in the continued
    dehumanization of a very human people.
No longer will we fulfill the prophecies layered
    upon us
throughout the generations of training and
    propaganda.
No longer will we hide the richness and beauty of
    our dark bodies.
No longer will we fail to claim the intelligence and
    creativity that are ours.
We give you back your self-loathing, self-sabotage,
    self-denial,

and claim the strength and power born of survival,
    born of centuries
of dead, unknown mothers and fathers, babies and
    siblings.
We give you back your segregation and separation.
We give you back your small gods and conditional
    hearts.
Today we throw down the chains of invisibility and
    tokenism,
the chains of acceptability and conformity.
Now is our time to thrive.

I had a slightly different experience with internalized oppression. As a child, I was raised with the deep brilliance of Black people and our history, resiliency, creativity, and physical beauty. My adoptive white mother would constantly point out the admirable qualities of Black women and men we saw and read about. Racism, I learned, was partly the result of the jealousy and inferiority that white people felt when in the presence of strong, exquisite Black people.

When the white people in my town would commit racist acts toward me, I internalized that I did not measure up to the other Black people in the world. I especially felt this way when other people of color called me "Oreo," or said that I wasn't really Black because of my family's racial make-up. I remember the deep pain I experienced in seminary when a Black woman minister told others that I didn't really know what it was to be Black because I was raised by white people.

I have had similar experiences with white people who said I wasn't really Black because I didn't "talk" or "act" Black—as if we all must talk and act in the same way. In my ministry, white people often forget or ignore that I am a Black woman dealing with white supremacy culture every day. Not "talking" or "acting" Black has not protected me from anti-Blackness and white supremacy. It has not prevented me from being pulled over by the police for driving while Black. It did not stop a white classmate from macing me as I walked behind her on a dimly lit street. It did not keep white people from calling me "nigger." It has not allowed me a seat at the proverbial table.

I have always loved being a Black woman. I have never thought, "I wish I were white." Though I have wished that I were more Black—darker skinned, more steeped in Black culture—and that I were a better Black person. The language of racism draws rigid lines between white and Black and brown people, creating boxes that few people fit in.

I Dream of Belonging

I dream of mahogany skin,
a shiny blackness that radiates from the soul;
a regal, full nose and high cheekbones
that cry out my African roots.
I dream of brown hands holding up my chin
telling me of a long, proud history of survival;
of queens and kings, of hunters and warriors,

of matriarchs and wise women.
I dream of dark roots buried deep in the rich earth,
holding my legs, supporting my spine,
so that I stand strong in the wake of my ancestors.
I dream of a community
of Black and brown women, men, and children,
nonbinary, and cis alike,
claiming me as one of their own, as kin,
calling me to them in celebration and welcome.
But then I awake
to the reality of life as it is:
to the loneliness of having a foot in many cultures
but belonging to none, all wanting me to be what I
    am not.
And tears of a lost dream fall.

Questions for Discussion

1. Internalized oppression does not just impact BIPOC, women, LGBTQ+ people, disabled people, poor and working-class people, or people of different body types and ages—we all internalize the stereotypes, prejudices, discrimination, and biases of white supremacy culture. What messages have you internalized that have prevented you from fully embracing who you are? How has this internalized oppression operated in your life?

2. What criteria do you use to classify a Black or brown person as Black or brown? Where did these criteria come from?

3. Historically speaking, how did people of color get classified and put into racial boxes?

Exercises

1. Think about when you have judged a person of color as *not* being a part of that cultural group. Write down why you did so.

2. Create a mantra of positive statements about yourself, and practice it three times a day for a week.

10

Our Time to Thrive

Indigenous people of the Americas, Africans forced through the Middle Passage, Asian communities facing exploitation and exoticization, and Latinx immigrants navigating borders have all survived unconscionable treatment at the hands of generations of white people. The continued ability of these communities to persevere, resist, and find joy, love, and a renewed hope in freedom is a miracle. As we have worked to shed the multiple chains and barriers of white supremacy, we have demanded a seat at the table, recognition of our gifts, and our time to thrive.

Scars and Stars

As I prepare to braid the soft mahogany wool of my
    niece's hair,
she asks me about the scars on my arms.
I take a deep breath, wondering what to say,
and continue to massage oil from a land we long
    abandoned into her scalp,

an excuse to put off the moment when her
    innocence about the world is marred.
Do I tell her about the manacles that rubbed so deep
    into our ancestor's bones
that the wounds remain visible even today?
Do I tell her about the lashes of the whips that were
    used to demean and control
by people who had no right to own us?
Can I explain the feel of the noose that a generation
    later
still causes me to wake at night in a sweat?
"Did someone hurt you?" she asks, unperturbed,
    and I wonder where to start.
These scars, I think, as I divide her hair into neat
    sections,
these burns and cut marks are simply skin
    imperfections—
scars that hide a lifetime of hurt and half-healings.
Do I tell her about the abuse, the discrimination, the
    dehumanization of our people?
They are the outer expressions of generations of
    survival, I think—
Generations of peoples who sought to thrive in the
    midst of hate;
who sought love in the midst of torment;
who sought life knowing that death was ever
    before them.
These scars come from the struggle to keep our heads
    up, our backs straight, our bodies moving.
They come from dancing through tears, singing
    through back-breaking, demeaning work,

smiling at the mere presence of a small, curious
    Black girl.
I want to tell her I was cut deep by a knife of
    oppression, burned in the fire of resistance.
But instead I lay my hand on her head and whisper,
"You are a part of the amazing bundle of life,
intricately connected with the land we walk upon,
with the air you share with your mother and with me,
and with all the ancestors who have lent their
    exhalations to future generations.
You are a precious, integral spark, born from stars,
loved not because of who you will become or how
    people treat you,
but just because you are."

The empowering history of Black and brown communities is one of perseverance, resistance, and hope—of staying the course in the face of tremendous challenges and with little or no guarantee of justice. This has never stopped us from sneaking into hidden woods and worshipping a God of deliverance, from wading into the water and following the North Star to a place of freedom, or from risking our lives to gain the right to vote or the right to simply be. We have organized and educated, marched and protested, as our houses were burned, our churches bombed, and our towns decimated. Black and brown people have persisted in the face of hatred, imprisonment, dehumanization, disease, and demeaning work and living conditions for a chance to live fully and freely in a world determined to not let us succeed. We are the people of hope — hope for a new day when we will be recognized for our intrinsic worth; hope for a day when we need not fear white fragility and power — a day where our presence and participation in the world will be celebrated and received with joy.

Hope

Hope is not just a thing with feathers
that lifts in good times and wilts in harsh weather.
It is a drum beat, a stomp, a hand firmly on the hip;
a sassy word, a determined lip.
It drives you out of bed when the will has left,
when the anger and pain leave you bereft.
It's the hustle at two jobs to keep the family fed
It is weary bones and weary spirits finally sinking
    into bed.
Hope is a new day when the possibilities are ripe,
when barriers shrink and energy lifts, draining all
    spite.
With curls swaying in the breeze and lotion on my
    elbows and knees,
I face the white world just as proud as you please.
And the smile on my brown sibling's face
lifts my heart to another space
of conviction and determination,
for in it is my salvation.
Cause no matter where my ambitions roam
with her walking with me, I am never alone.

Black and brown communities have had to use basic tools to survive, handed down from grandparent to parent to child: if you are pulled over by the police, keep your hands visible, look straight ahead, do not talk back, say "yes, sir" and "no, sir," and announce when you are reaching for your wallet and registration. Do not walk, drive, or linger in predominantly or all-white neighborhoods. Learn to code-switch, and talk, walk, and dress as white people do. Do not laugh or talk too loudly or express too much anger in front of white people.

Other strategies of resistance have centered around physical and creative outlets as ways to connect with community, family, and the ancestors while exorcising the toxicity of racism. From the plains, deserts, woods and mountains of Africa, the Americas, and the Islands; on the boats laden with chains; across the deserts and through the tunnels; and in the midst of slaughter, disease, and forced separations, Black and brown people have stomped and danced; clapped and sung; painted, woven, and sculpted; and played games to soothe our spirits and recharge our energy.

Sold into physically demanding and demeaning work, enslaved Black people and their descendants turned to music for comfort. They sang while picking cotton and tobacco leaves, on long marches and breaks in the military, on chain gangs, in prison, and in church when allowed to attend (and in secret when they were not). Formerly enslaved abolitionist Frederick Douglass wrote of his captivity, "We were remarkably buoyant, singing hymns and making joyous exclamations, almost as triumphant in their tone as if we had already reached a land of freedom and safety."

Because the immediate obstacle for multicultural captives from Africa was an inability to speak the same language, enslaved Africans employed the same tools in forming their new tribal identity as they had in their communities of origin. They came together in ceremonies of song and dance. Representing a fundamentally spiritual celebration of life, song and dance continue to be the way in which many African, African American, and Black communities affirm our relationship to the forces to which we owe our existence. These ritual ceremonies began as emotional shouts and moans, in which music, hand gestures, movement and rhythm were more important than words. Eventually, the shouts and moans developed into a language specific to enslaved African communities—songs we now call spirituals.

The lyrics of spirituals emerged from the everyday experiences of slavery. Many spoke of the injustice, pain, anger, and anguish that our enslaved ancestors needed to express. In the singing of such songs, enslaved people began the transformative process of constructing methods of survival and perseverance in a life determined to dehumanize them. Through words and movement, they lifted themselves in pride and power. The spirituals wept out their grief, shouted out their anger, and fought for their lives.

For many communities of color, dancing has had similar effects. For me, dancing is a spiritual and therapeutic act. When I can let go and allow my body to flow with the rhythm, I am transported to another place of connection, joy, and release.

The Dance of the Drum

The beat of the drum echoes in my heart,
reverberating in my soul and pulsing through my
    veins.
Its persistent call draws me from within myself
and without conscious thought, my head bobs in
    assent.
As the music swells within me, I have no choice;
I must move my hands, my feet, my hips, my arms—
tentatively at first, as if waking up and throwing off
    cobwebs of sleep.
Ignoring the shackles of conformity and propriety—
    I move
Shedding the disappointments and discouragements
    of the day—I move
Letting go of the anxiety of living a life of brown
    and Blackness—I move
Feeling the energy of generations of my African
    ancestors,
generations of my enslaved, colonized, and
    decimated kin,
the generations who resisted, who survived,

whose tears joined with mine—I move.
And then a joy so complete overtakes me
and I give myself up to the rhythms,
letting my body lead and my mind still,
stomping, swaying, clapping with abandon.
My soul takes flight and I laugh out loud—
a laugh that is as nourishing as any meal could be.
Although the drums eventually cease,
the dance echoes in my bones, and like the smell
    of burning leaves,
it lingers on my smile long after the silence
    descends.

I remember a classmate asking me why Black people haven't prospered like other immigrants in the US when we have been free for over two hundred years. Our teacher had failed to mention that Black people were not, for the most part, immigrants. We were taken in chains from Africa and sold like cattle to be abused in the homes of and on lands usurped by white people.

A Dream Worth Waking To

I dream of freedom—an unbound life.
As one often does when life isn't your own—
when other people hold the chains, the keys to the
    locks,
the end of the rope that binds your body, your spirit . . .

It is not the work or the lash or the living conditions
    that take pieces of your soul.
It is that eventually, if they are clever and you,
    susceptible,
  they bind your mind.
And your ability to distinguish their wants from your
    own diminishes.
And your strength to resist their disdain fades.
And your dreams of freedom, of flying untethered
  wherever your imagination can take you
die, in a pale, uncrossable desert, without water or
    nourishment or hope.
And how can you be free while carrying the dead
of those who could not make the trek, who became
    sacrifices
  for your chance at safety and self-determination?
How can you truly be free when the forty years of
    wilderness stretch to four hundred,
when the journey seems too long, the cost too high,
    and your will too broken?
Is it possible, after all this time, to throw down the
    chains of bondage
but remain bound by the silken threads of divine
    webbing?
Is it possible, after all the hate, all the hubris, all the
    wrenching pain
to let go of the reins, to shed the chains, to find
    freedom in one another?
Impossible—yes.
And yet, I think, the only dream worth waking to.

The musician K. Longer wrote a powerful song, "We Shall Be Known," whose lyrics include, "It is time now. It is time now that we thrive." Black and brown people have survived disease, genocide, slavery, lynchings, home and church burnings, tar and feathering, rapes and beatings, segregation, the deliberate flooding of drugs and disease into our communities, humiliation, silencing, caging, inequality, scapegoating—in sum, hundreds of years of systematic dehumanization. Surviving is not enough anymore. The time is now! It is time that we thrive.

Questions for Discussion

1. Were there periods in your life when you felt like you were just surviving? What did you draw upon to get through?

2. Imagine that you are Sisyphus rolling a boulder up the hill, and every time you almost reach the top, the boulder slips and rolls back down. What would motivate you to keep trying to get the boulder over the hill?

3. What has our society indoctrinated in you that you would rather reject?

4. What is your dream for our country? How do you plan to help realize that dream?

Exercises

1. Write a story about resilience and what it takes to keep working for justice in a white supremacist culture.

2. If you're white and haven't already, read *How to Be an Antiracist* by Ibram X. Kendi. List action steps you can take to help dismantle white supremacy.

3. Write your resistance poem—the poem that keeps you pushing forward even when you want to give up.